Art Center College Library
1700 Lida St.
Pasadena, CA 91103

D1051961

ART CENTER COLLEGE OF DESIGN

3 3220 00232 2100

796.830924
A 398
L 834
2006

ALI RAP

DISCARD

MUHAMMAD ALI
THE FIRST
HEAVYWEIGHT CHAMPION
OF RAP

EDITED AND DESIGNED
BY GEORGE LOIS

To Lonnie Ali

MUHAMMAD ALI, WHEN ASKED
WHAT HIS WIFE MEANS TO HIM:

"*Everything.*"

Before there was Rap (before there was even Rock) there was
Ali Rap...a topsy-turvy, jivey jargon that only Ali could create, but
a language we could all understand. Talk about an original!
Way back at the age of 12, a white Louisville cop gave him boxing
lessons so he could whup the guy who stole his bike—in six weeks,
as an aspiring prizefighter, the 89-pound Cassius rapped his first poem
predicting "This guy is done. I'll stop him in one." And from
then on, the flow was nonstop. His chatter. His poems. His predictions.
His uproarious use of language soared, even as his fabulous
life unfolded, taking him past boxing, beyond race, until he became...
and remains...the most famous human on our planet.
Inspired by the showbiz wrestler Gorgeous George, Ali introduced
the persona of the extroverted, romantic egomaniac to the
legitimate American sports scene. Before Ali, you had Babe Ruth,
who (allegedly) called his shot by pointing his bat toward
the faraway fence. Ali spent his entire career predicting what time
lightning would strike in each bout, and in rhyme!

When a brash Cassius Clay befuddled and then battered Sonny Liston
(The Shock Heard 'Round the World) he not only changed all
of sports forever, he went on to change America. He drew his strength
from being Black, from being a Muslim, from Allah, from being
a rebel who opposed the Vietnam War, from being loved by the poorest
of the poor, from spending time with kids in the 'hood, from
visiting Jewish old-age homes, earning him the right to be called
a leader of his people—a blast furnace of racial pride!
His whole life was an Ali Rope-a-Dope: a loudmouth windbag and,

at the same time, a sincere, dedicated and disciplined athlete;
a man who was a sucker for every sad story, yet a vicious bully in the
ring; a prissy puritan, totally intolerant of boozers and smokers,
but at times a wash-your-mouth-out-with-soap raconteur of dirty jokes.

Muhammad Ali was the heavyweight champion of everything:
hype, PR, media, showbiz, street theater, black humor, moneymaking,
politics, rap, the greatest boxing champion ever, and certainly
the superstar to end all superstars, the epitome of superstardom—
The Greatest. A pugilistic jester whose verbal jabs made more
headlines than his punches in the ring, his doggerel was an upscale
version of street trash talk, the first time whites had ever heard
such versifying—becoming the first rapper, the precursor to Tupac and
Jay-Z. His first-person rhymes and rhythms extolling his hubris
were hilarious hip-hop, decades before Run-D.M.C., Rakim and
LL Cool J. His style, his desecrating mouth, his beautiful
irrationality, his principled, even prophetic stand against the Vietnam
War, all added to his
credentials as a true-born
slayer of authority,
and the most beloved man
of our time.

MUHAMMAD ALI
& GEORGE LOIS, 1968

INTRODUCTION by Ron Holland

Any champion...certainly any heavyweight champion...can bring
us to our feet...bring us to cheers...and sometimes, bring us
to tears. But damn it, one...and only one...made us laugh. Right.
Out. Loud. That's him. Muhammad Ali. The man who rapped
before they called it Rap. Impossibly good looking. With a body
Michelangelo might have sculpted, to give us a black David.
And blessed with a blend of boxing skills that no heavyweight...
not even the idolized Joe Louis...ever possessed. Dancing,
darting, debonair and devilish...rapping in the face of every great
contender of his time. And you don't know the half of it.
He was funnier than you'll ever know. Unless and until you flip
to any page of this book.

During the dark period of Ali's exile, George Lois, a Greek florist's kid
from the Bronx, Korean War veteran, defiant maverick, legendary
ad man and provocateur graphic designer, helped energize support
for the convicted fighter by creating three impactful covers
for the mass magazine *Esquire*, all protesting the banishment of
Muhammad Ali for refusing to fight in an unjust war
(political heresy in America at that time).

After that terrible wrong was righted in 1971, when the Supreme
Court threw out Ali's conviction as a draft-dodger, Lois
designed the outrageous Ali/Frazier III closed-circuit fight program,
as well as enlisted Ali, an active symbol of peace and
reconciliation, to publicly lead a propaganda war against the legal
authorities of New Jersey to free the innocent Rubin 'Hurricane'

Carter, a victim of racial injustice. Cassius Clay, the boxer who had stunned the world with his dazzling fists, outrageous footwork, audacious rhymes and passion for life, had now, as Muhammad Ali, become popular among whites, and a godlike figure to blacks.

Baseball Hall of Famer Reggie Jackson made this acute observation: "Ali helped raise black people in this country out of mental slavery. The entire experience of being black changed for millions of people because of Ali." This book vividly documents, in Muhammad Ali's own words, his passion and fighting spirit that helped change the despair of a bad, bad time in America.

For half his lifetime, George Lois has kept his ear cocked for examples of Ali rap and rapture, and has indelibly preserved and transformed them with his astonishing visual spin. And whether Ali is proving to the world he can write the world's shortest poem, or dissecting the tissue of bigotry in America, or deftly jiggling the math to make a

knockout prediction come true, you, and whoever you share this hilarious, and often moving marriage of words and pictures with, will delight in the wonderful world of Ali Rap.

MUHAMMAD ALI
& GEORGE LOIS, 2003

Cassius Marcellus Clay Jr.
Born January 17, 1942,
in the West End section, a black
ghetto in Louisville, Kentucky,
during the days of
Southern Jim Crow laws

"Gee-Gee, Gee-Gee."

*THE FIRST SOUNDS FROM CASSIUS CLAY
WHEN HE WAS A BABY–
HIS MOTHER, ODESSA CLAY, CALLED HIM
'G-G' FOR THE REST OF HER LIFE*

*"After I won the Golden Gloves,
I told Mama Bird that
from the very beginning I was trying
to say 'Golden Gloves.'"*

"The first person I ever knocked out was my mom."

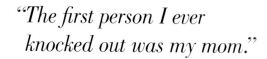

BABY CASSIUS ACCIDENTALLY HIT HIS MOTHER IN THE MOUTH, LOOSENING TWO FRONT TEETH THAT HAD TO BE PULLED.

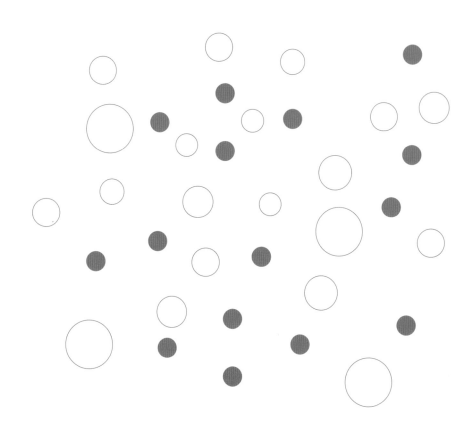

"My mama told me
I was always in a hurry as a child.
I even had measles and
chicken pox at the same time."

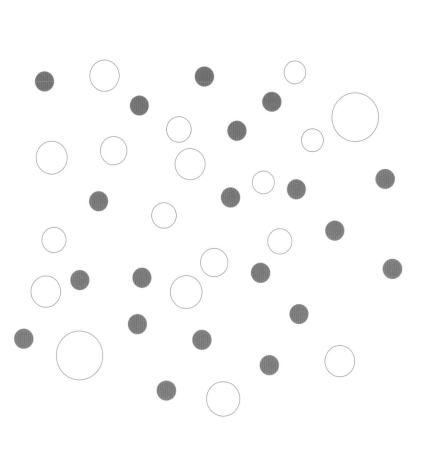

IN 1954, CASSIUS CLAY SR. SURPRISED
HIS SON WITH A SPIFFY
NEW $60 RED-AND-WHITE SCHWINN.
IT WAS PROMPTLY STOLEN–
A PIVOTAL MOMENT IN THE LIFE OF THE
FUTURE MUHAMMAD ALI!

12-year-old, 89-pound Cassius Clay:
"I'm gonna whup whoever stole my bike!"

Louisville policeman Joe Martin:
"Well, you better learn how to fight before you start challenging people that you're gonna whup!"

JOE MARTIN TRAINED YOUNG BOXERS IN HIS SPARE TIME–
SIX MONTHS LATER, CASSIUS MADE HIS RING DEBUT
AND WON A THREE-ROUND DECISION

"I used to ask my brother Rudy to throw rocks at me. He thought I was crazy but I'd dodge every one of them. That's how I learned how to bob and weave: ducking rocks."

"This guy is done. I'll stop him in one."

12-YEAR-OLD CASSIUS CLAY'S
FIRST RAP PREDICTION,
PRINTED IN THE
LOUISVILLE COURIER-JOURNAL, 1954

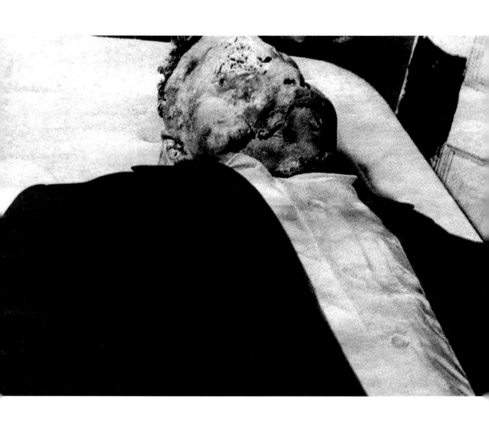

"When I was 13,
I saw a newspaper with
a front-page story about a boy named
Emmett Till. He was a black
boy about the same age as me, who was
brutalized and lynched
while on vacation in Mississippi,
supposedly for whistling
at a white woman. A picture of him
in his coffin was in the paper,
with a gruesome description of what
had been done to him.
It made me sick, and it scared me."

EMMETT'S MOTHER MADE THE COURAGEOUS DECISION
TO OPEN HER SON'S CASKET AT A MASS FUNERAL
IN CHICAGO, FOR ALL THE WORLD TO SEE
(ALTHOUGH THE PHOTOGRAPH WAS TOTALLY SHUNNED
BY WHITE MEDIA THROUGHOUT AMERICA).
BUT THE TWO WHITE KILLERS WERE ACQUITTED
BY AN ALL-WHITE, ALL-MALE JURY IN MISSISSIPPI,
BUT LATER ADMITTED TO THEIR GUILT
IN A STORY THEY SOLD TO LOOK MAGAZINE.

"You can get hurt playing football!"

*WHEN ASKED WHY HE NEVER
PLAYED FOOTBALL IN HIS YOUTH*

*Y.A. TITTLE, 1964,
IN A SEMINAL PHOTO THAT
ICONIZED THE BRUTAL
NATURE OF PRO FOOTBALL
IN AMERICA*

**"I'm young,
I'm handsome,
I'm fast,
I'm pretty
and can't possibly be beat.
They must fall
in the round I call."**

16-YEAR-OLD
CASSIUS MARCELLUS CLAY JR.
AKA: THE LOUISVILLE LIP
     MIGHTY MOUTH
     THE MARVELOUS MOUTH
     GASEOUS CASSIUS
     CASH THE BRASH
     CLAPTRAP CLAY
     BLABBERMOUTH

*"My name is Cassius Marcellus Clay Jr.
I have won six Golden Gloves tournaments
in Kentucky. I have fought in the
Tournament of Champions in Chicago.
I won the National Amateur Athletic Union
Championship in Toledo and I am the 1959
National Golden Gloves Light Heavyweight
Champion. And I'm going to win the
gold medal in the 1960 Rome Olympics."*

Angelo Dundee (TO HIS FIGHTER, WILLIE PASTRANO):
*"Willie, there's some kinda nut downstairs,
wants to talk to me."*

Willie Pastrano:
"There's nothing good on TV so send him up."

> *"How can he talk like that?*
> *Ain't he gonna get in trouble?"*

ON HIS FIRST TRIP TO NEW YORK AFTER LIVING
HIS YOUTH IN THE JIM CROW SOUTH, BEFORE GOING
TO ROME TO COMPETE IN THE 1960 OLYMPICS,
A NAIVE 18-YEAR-OLD CASSIUS CLAY SAW A BLACK
MAN IN HARLEM STANDING UP AND ADVOCATING
RESISTANCE TO WHITE AMERICA.

"Sugar Ray was the kind of boxer I wanted to be. Before I left for Italy for the Olympics, I tried to reach Sugar Ray. I walked all the way up Fifth Avenue to 125th Street. I wanted to tell him that I admired him and that I was going to be the heavyweight champion of the world by the time I was 21. When I arrived at Sugar Ray's club I waited outside all day. I would have stood outside all week if I had to. It was about 10 o'clock when he finally showed up. I was so excited that for the first time in my life I was speechless. When I pulled myself together, I walked up to Mr. Robinson and told him how far I had come just to see him and that he was my hero. He never looked at me. He said 'Later, boy, I'm busy right now.' I just stood there as I watched Sugar Ray Robinson turn his back on me and walk away. At that moment, I vowed never to turn a fan away."

"To make America the greatest is my goal,
So I beat the Russian and I beat the Pole,
And for the USA won the medal of gold.
Italy said, 'You're greater than Cassius of Old,
We like your name, we like your game,
So make Rome your home if you will.'
I said I appreciate kind hospitality,
But the USA is my country still,
'Cause they're waiting to welcome me
in Louisville."

*"First time in my life
I ever slept on my back.
Had to, or the medal
would have hurt my chest!"*

ON RETURNING HOME FROM ROME,
CASSIUS WORE HIS 1960 OLYMPIC
LIGHT HEAVYWEIGHT GOLD MEDAL
DAY AND NIGHT.

Cassius Clay Cassius Clay Cassius Clay Cassius Clay
Cassius Clay Cassius Clay Cassius Clay Cassius Clay
Cassius Clay Cassius Clay Cassius Clay Cassius Clay
Cassius Clay Cassius Clay Cassius Clay Cassius Clay
Cassius Clay Cassius Clay Cassius Clay Cassius Clay
Cassius Clay Cassius Clay Cassius Clay Cassius Clay
Cassius Clay Cassius Clay Cassius Clay Cassius Clay
Cassius Clay Cassius Clay Cassius Clay Cassius Clay
Cassius Clay Cassius Clay Cassius Clay Cassius Clay
Cassius Clay Cassius Clay Cassius Clay Cassius Clay
Cassius Clay Cassius Clay Cassius Clay Cassius Clay
Cassius Clay Cassius Clay Cassius Clay Cassius Clay
Cassius Clay Cassius Clay Cassius Clay Cassius Clay
Cassius Clay Cassius Clay Cassius Clay Cassius Clay
Cassius Clay Cassius Clay Cassius Clay Cassius Clay
Cassius Clay Cassius Clay Cassius Clay Cassius Clay
Cassius Clay Cassius Clay Cassius Clay Cassius Clay
Cassius Clay Cassius Clay Cassius Clay Cassius Clay
Cassius Clay Cassius Clay Cassius Clay Cassius Clay
Cassius Clay Cassius Clay Cassius Clay Cassius Clay
Cassius Clay Cassius Clay Cassius Clay Cassius Clay
Cassius Clay Cassius Clay Cassius Clay Cassius Clay
Cassius Clay Cassius Clay Cassius Clay Cassius Clay
Cassius Clay Cassius Clay Cassius Clay Cassius Clay
Cassius Clay Cassius Clay Cassius Clay Cassius Clay
Cassius Clay Cassius Clay Cassius Clay Cassius Clay
Cassius Clay Cassius Clay Cassius Clay Cassius Clay
Cassius Clay Cassius Clay Cassius Clay Cassius Clay
Cassius Clay Cassius Clay Cassius Clay Cassius Clay

"I love to see my name in print."

*"The man said, 'We don't serve Negroes.'
I said, 'I don't eat them either!'
They shouted, 'Boy, get out!'
I looked at my gold medal and thought,
'This thing ain't worth nothin'–
it can't even get me a hamburger!'"*

*19-YEAR-OLD OLYMPIC GOLD WINNER
CASSIUS CLAY IN MIAMI*

"I saw 15,000 people coming to see this man get beat. And his talking did it. I said, 'This is a gooood idea!'"

WATCHING THE LEGENDARY WRESTLER GORGEOUS GEORGE PERFORM CAME AS A SHOWBIZ EPIPHANY TO THE YOUNG CASSIUS CLAY

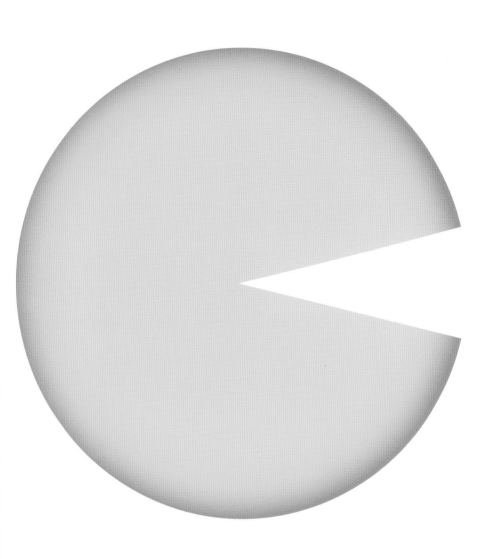

> *"Do you have to eat the whole thing, or can I buy just one piece?"*

CASSIUS CLAY LOOKING LONGINGLY
AT A LARGE CHEESECAKE ON DISPLAY
AT JACK DEMPSEY'S RESTAURANT
JUST AFTER HIS 1960 OLYMPICS VICTORY

*WHILE BEING ALLOWED
TO TRAIN IN ARCHIE MOORE'S
CAMP EARLY IN HIS CAREER,
CASSIUS RESPONDED TO ARCHIE'S
REQUEST HE DO CHORES:*

*"Archie,
I didn't come here to be
a dishwasher."*

Old Dutch
Cleanser

Chases
Dirt

MAKES EVERYTHING "SPICK AND SPAN"

Keeps all
Cooking and Kitchen
Utensils
Spotless and Sanitary
saves time, money and labor

"I'm beautiful. Beeeoootiful.
I'm the greatest.
I'm the double-fastest.
I'm clean and sparkling.
I will be a clean
and sparkling champion."

*"The only thing I ever did like drugs
was twice I took the cap off
a gas tank and smelled the gas,
which made me dizzy.
Never again!"*

"**M**y face is so pretty,
You don't see a scar,
Which proves I'm the king
Of the ring by far."

"I'll go dancin' with Johansson."

BEFORE HIS FIRST PRO FIGHT, WHEN CASSIUS
WAS OFFERED THE CHANCE TO SPAR WITH
HEAVYWEIGHT CHAMPION INGEMAR JOHANSSON

"Come on, sucka, what's the matter?
Can't you catch me?
I'm the one who should be fighting
Patterson, not you!"

THE OUTCLASSED SWEDE'S TRAINER
MERCIFULLY ENDED THE SESSION AFTER
TWO ROUNDS.

"After four
You can head for the door
And if he tries to get rough–
One's enough."

IN 1960, BEFORE FIGHTING
HERBERT SILER, HIS SECOND PRO FIGHT
(CASSIUS MADE GOOD
HIS 4ᵀᴴ ROUND PREDICTION)

"There are a lot of boys that are stronger than me that could be great champions, but they can't fight temptation. Temptation is all around us! Pretty girls with their chests big and ripe."

Me,
Whe

eee!

ON THE TONIGHT SHOW, *CASSIUS CLAY PROVES*
THAT HE CAN CREATE A TWO-WORD POEM

©FLIP SCHULKE

*"Do you know why
I'm the fastest heavyweight
in the world?
I'm the only heavyweight
that trains underwater!"*

*CASSIUS CLAY (WHO COULDN'T SWIM)
CONNING PHOTOGRAPHER FLIP SCHULKE TO
SHOOT "EXCLUSIVE" PHOTOS OF HIM,
SUPPOSEDLY TRAINING UNDERWATER
(ANGELO DUNDEE WAS THERE
TO MAKE SURE CASSIUS DIDN'T DROWN)*

123456

*"They must fall
In the round I call!"*

"Float like a butterfly,

Sting like a bee
Your hands can't hit
What your eyes can't see."

"Rumble, young man, rumble, aaaahh!"

DREW 'BUNDINI' BROWN

*"I felt this cool breeze
one night in a dream.
Then I heard a door slam.
Then this voice:*

"IN FOOOUR!"

(SOUNDING LIKE LOU COSTELLO IMITATING DRACULA)

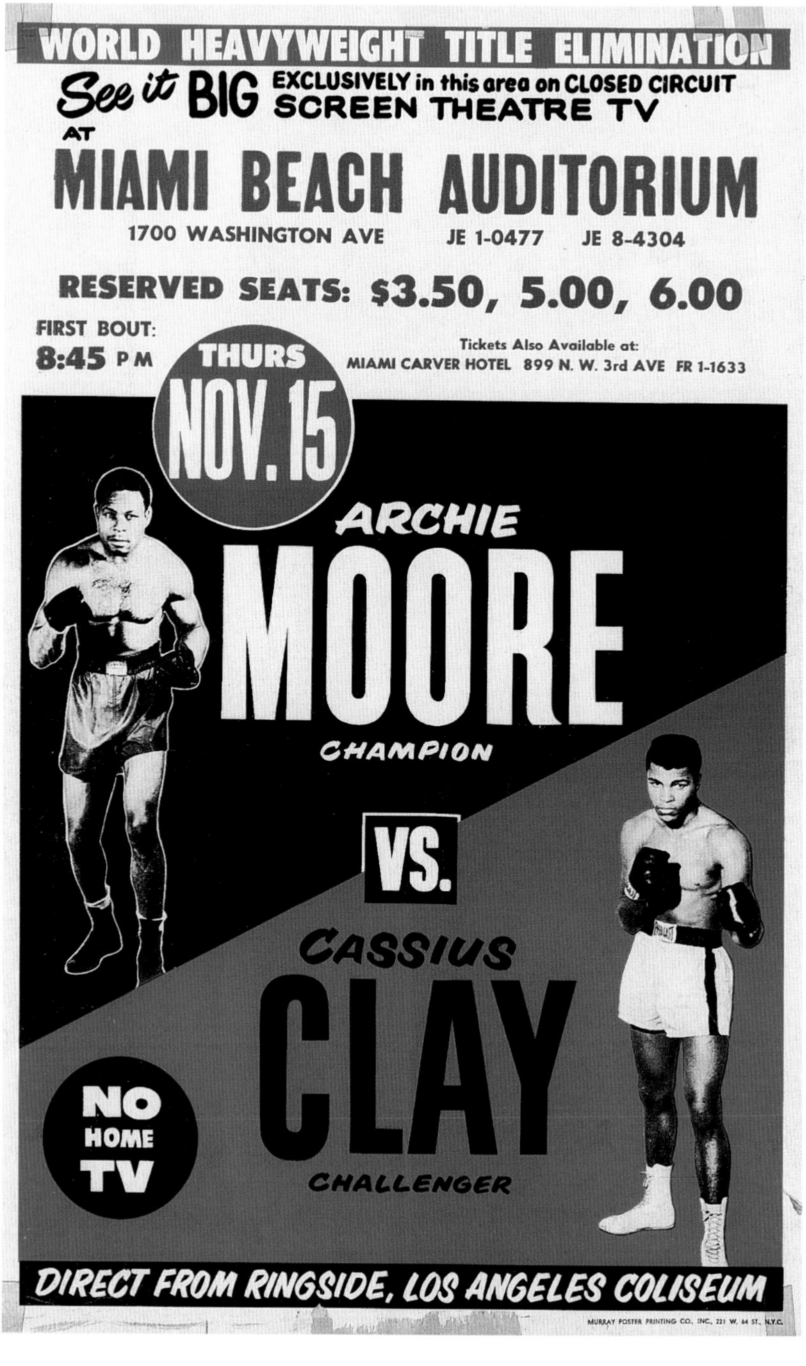
WORLD HEAVYWEIGHT TITLE ELIMINATION
See it BIG EXCLUSIVELY in this area on CLOSED CIRCUIT SCREEN THEATRE TV
AT
MIAMI BEACH AUDITORIUM
1700 WASHINGTON AVE JE 1-0477 JE 8-4304
RESERVED SEATS: $3.50, 5.00, 6.00
FIRST BOUT: 8:45 PM
THURS NOV. 15
Tickets Also Available at:
MIAMI CARVER HOTEL 899 N. W. 3rd AVE FR 1-1633
ARCHIE
MOORE
CHAMPION
VS.
CASSIUS
CLAY
CHALLENGER
NO HOME TV
DIRECT FROM RINGSIDE, LOS ANGELES COLISEUM
MURRAY POSTER PRINTING CO., INC., 221 W. 64 ST., N.Y.C.

"When you come to the fight
Don't block the halls
And don't block the door
For y'all may go home
After round four.

He was old and I was new.
And you could tell
By the blows I threw.
I swept that old man
Clean out of the ring–
For a new broom sweeps
'Most anything.

Archie's been living
Off the fat of the land–
I'm here to give him his
Pension plan."

"*When I was a young fighter,*
I had to KO Anthony Quinn,
playing Mountain Rivera,
a washed-up fighter.

When I saw the movie,
I felt so sorry for him."

REFERRING TO HIS MOVIE ROLE IN
REQUIEM FOR A HEAVYWEIGHT

*"Where do you think I would be
if I didn't shout and holler?
I would be poor and down in Louisville
washing windows, shining shoes
or running an elevator and saying
'Yes suh' and 'No suh,'
and knowing my place."*

The NEWSBOYS' AND BOOTBLACKS'

Minstrel Show

Price One Dollar

T. S. DENISON & COMPANY - Publishers - Minneapolis, Minn.

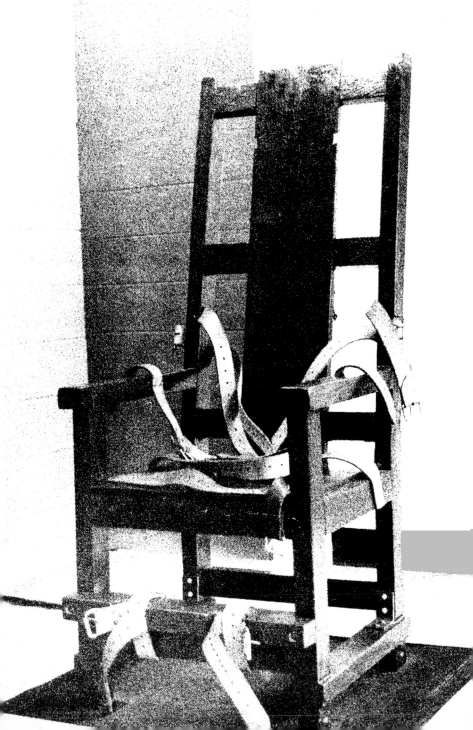

"You crazy, man.
You can get electrocuted for that—
a Jew looking at a white girl
in Kentucky."

JUST AFTER DICK SCHAAP POINTED OUT
THE BEAUTY OF A YOUNG LADY IN LOUISVILLE

"To get a good gate,
I wear those pretty white shoes
and those shiny white trunks
and the women says,
'Land, ain't he nice and neat.'
The women don't like
the sight of blood, either,
so I make sure they
never see none of mine
by not gettin' hit."

Art Center College Library
1700 Lida St.
Pasadena, CA 91103

"I want to see my beautiful Technicolor face on the cover of LIFE!"

CASSIUS CLAY, THREE YEARS BEFORE MAKING THE COVER OF LIFE AS MUHAMMAD ALI, THE NEW HEAVYWEIGHT CHAMPION OF THE WORLD. (THE COVER SHOWN IS CAPTIONED "CASSIUS CLAY," BUT IS ONE OF HIS FIRST AUTOGRAPHS AS "MUHAMMAD ALI")

LIFE

CASSIUS
CLAY

MARCH 6 1964 · 25¢

"When I was a young fighter,
I was booked into a suite at the Waldorf,
right next to the Prince of Wales.
I never heard of him, but he was famous,
so I knocked on the door, and the
butler answered and said:
'We have not requested room service.'"

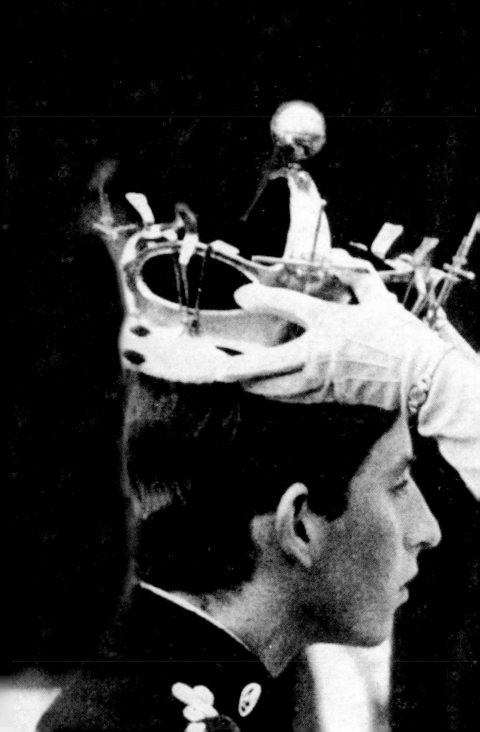

"I don't pretend to be friendly,
like most people do
when they're trying to get to the top.
I AM friendly."

JULIUS CAESAR,
46 B.C.

"Marcellus vanquished Carthage,
Cassius laid Julius Caesar low,
And Clay will flatten Doug Jones,
With a mighty muscled blow,
So when the gong rings
And the referee sings out 'The Winner,'
Cassius Marcellus Clay
Will be the noblest Roman of them all."

FIGHT OF
YEAR - NO TELEVISION
SQ. GARDEN
Ave. 49th & 50th Sts.
WED. MAR. 13
8:30 P. M.
MAIN EVENT — 10 ROUNDS
CASSIUS
CLAY
Sensational Fast Talking, Fast Punching Undefeated Young Heavyweight Contender, Rated No. 2. Former U. S. Olympic
VS
DOUG
JONES
York Challenger For World's Heavyweight
SEMI-FINAL
VS

"Jones like to mix
So I'll let it go six
If he talks jive
I'll cut it to five
And if he talks some more
I'll cut it to four
And if he talks about me
I'll cut it to three
And if that don't do
I'll cut it to two
And if you want some fun
I'll cut it to one
And if he don't want to fight
He can stay home that night."

"I decided on six.
Now I'm changing the pick I made before,
Instead of six, Doug goes in four."

WHEN HE WON A 10-ROUND DECISION AGAINST DOUG JONES:

*"Well, first I said six,
then I said four–
that adds up to ten!"*

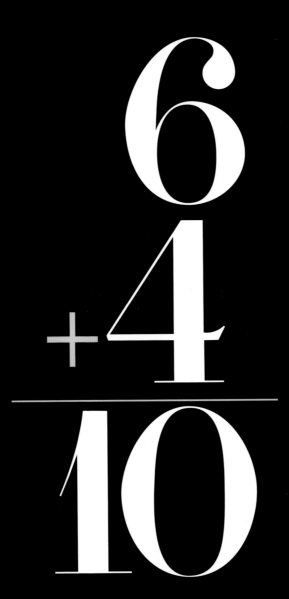

"When you're goin' good, man,
they fall out of the sky—
it rains pretty foxes."

Cassius:
"What are these things?"

Craps croupier:
"Chips, chips."

Cassius:

"*Don't gimme none of that stuff.*
Gimme some more of those silver dollars."

YOUNG CASSIUS THREW DICE IN LAS VEGAS IN 1963,
SO IGNORANT OF CRAPS HE COMPLAINED
WHEN HE WAS GIVEN CASINO CHIPS AFTER
A WINNING ROLL.

"This time I'm even a bigger fool,
Flat on my back instead of a stool."

*AN EMBARRASSED CASSIUS CLAY, KNOCKED DOWN
BY HENRY COOPER FOR THE FIRST TIME IN HIS CAREER*

"I was momentarily distracted when I saw Cleopatra."

EXPLAINING WHY, WHEN HE GLIMPSED ELIZABETH TAYLOR SITTING AT RINGSIDE IN LONDON, HENRY COOPER KNOCKED HIM DOWN. (THERE WERE SPORTSWRITERS AT RINGSIDE WHO ACTUALLY CORROBORATED CLAY'S STORY!) BUT CASSIUS KO'd COOPER THE NEXT ROUND, AS PREDICTED.

"*Life is a gamble.*
You can get hurt, but people
die in plane crashes,
lose their arms and legs in car accidents;
people die every day.
Same with fighters: Some die,
some get hurt, some go on.
You just don't let yourself believe
it will happen to you."

"Come here, all you beautiful black children."

*CASSIUS WOULD DRIVE UP TO SCHOOLYARDS AT RECESS AND
GATHER DOZENS OF ADORING KIDS AROUND HIM (HERE LOVINGLY
PHOTOGRAPHED WITH MALCOLM X BY HOWARD L. BINGHAM,
HIS EVER-PRESENT PHOTOGRAPHER AND FRIEND).*

"Man, it was a really a letdown drag
For all those miles I had to eat out of a bag."

DESCRIBING A CAR TRIP FROM MIAMI TO NEW YORK IN 1964 WHEN HE WAS RESTRICTED FROM WHITE RESTAURANTS IN THE JIM CROW SOUTH

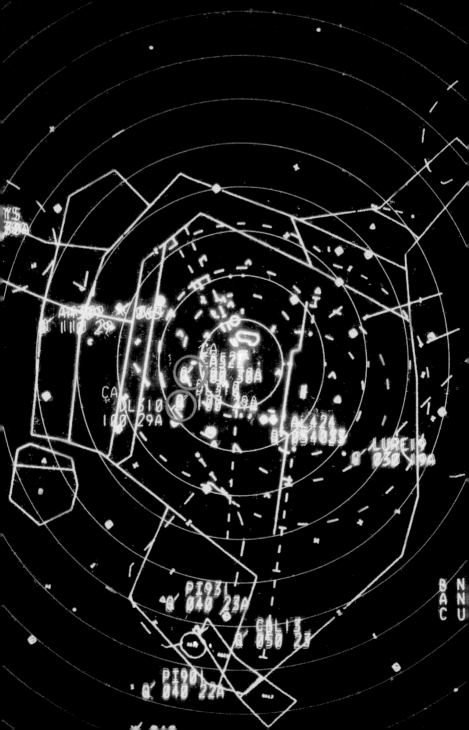

*"I have a radar built inside me
to avoid punches."*

"**I**'m just another nigger,

Trying to be bigger."

A SELF-DEPRECATING
RIFF ON RACE ALWAYS RECEIVED
HOWLS OF LAUGHTER
FROM AFRICAN-AMERICAN FANS

*"I might not be welcome.
And besides, I don't believe
in forcing integration.
You go ahead, though,
Jackie Robinson."*

*"I figured that if I said it enough,
I would convince the world
that I really WAS the greatest!"*

"I'm a young man, y'know,
in the prime of life.
With all the temptations,
I have to resist.
But I don't even kiss none,
because you get
too close, it's almost impossible
to stop there."

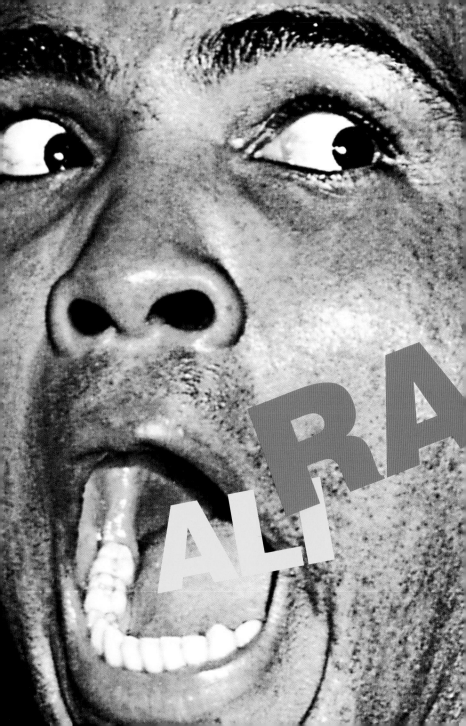

*"All the time I gotta talk, y'know.
People expect it.
Reporters say, 'We don't want to ask you
questions, man—just talk!'
My mouth is tired!"*

"One good thing about a bus: If it breaks down, it don't fall 30,000 feet."

CASSIUS CLAY PREFERRED TRAVELING IN HIS OWN 1953 FLXIBLE 30-PASSENGER BUS

Favorite movie: "Shane"
Favorite song: "'I Can't Stand It' by James Brow*
Favorite singer: "Elvis"
Favorite fighter: "Jack Johnson"
Favorite food: "Lamb chops (and bean pie)"
Favorite candy: "Baby Ruth,
and that's the truth!"*

Ruth.

OZ. (39 Grams)

AFTER SPRUCING UP HIS WHITE BOOTS
PRIOR TO A BOUT, HE LEFT
HIS LOCKER ROOM TO WALK TO THE RING,
BUT WENT BACK TO COMB HIS HAIR:

"There's girls out there."

*"I eat fighting
and I drink
fighting.
I fight when I'm
in the shower.
And I even
talk fighting
when I'm
with women."*

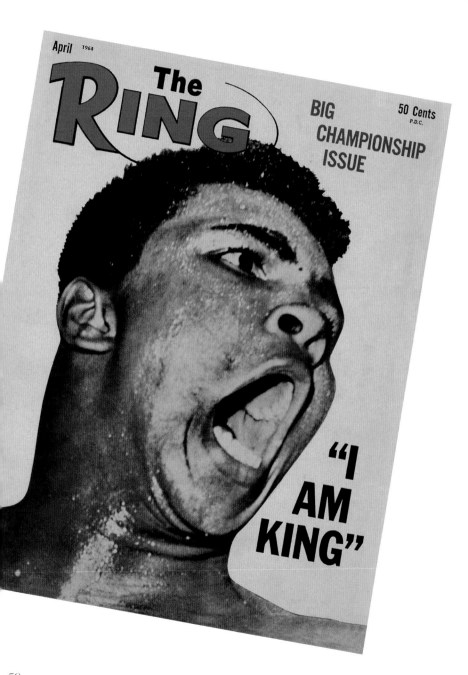

59

*"You got a queen, you need a king.
I am King!"*

*CASSIUS CLAY, TO THE PEOPLE
OF ENGLAND BEFORE HIS SECOND FIGHT
WITH HENRY COOPER*

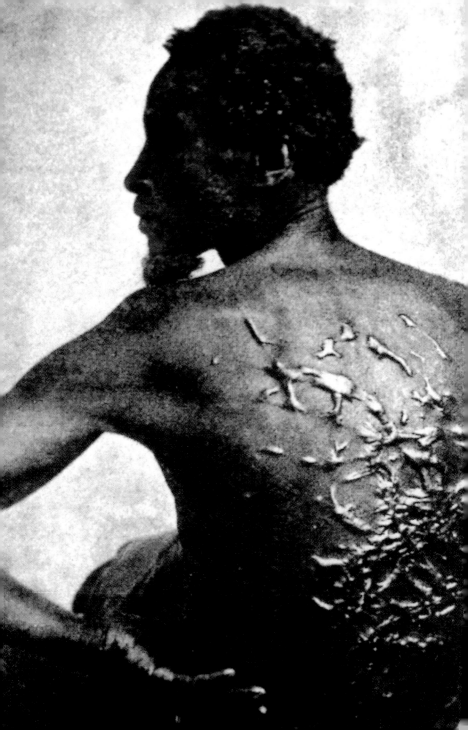

"Every time I think of the times when my ancestors were slaves of the white man, I cry."

"Blackbirds fly with blackbirds.
You don't mix apples and oranges."

"What does the white man care
if I hate him, anyhow?
He's got everything going for him—
White Swan soap, Tarzan is white,
Jesus is white, White Owl cigars,
the White Tornado, Snow White and
her Seven Dwarfs...the White House!
Angel food cake is all white.
But Devil's food cake is black!"

"Nothing is wrong..

But something ain't rigdt."

THE WARY PHILOSOPHY OF A YOUNG
AFRICAN-AMERICAN
GROWING UP IN A RACIST AMERICA

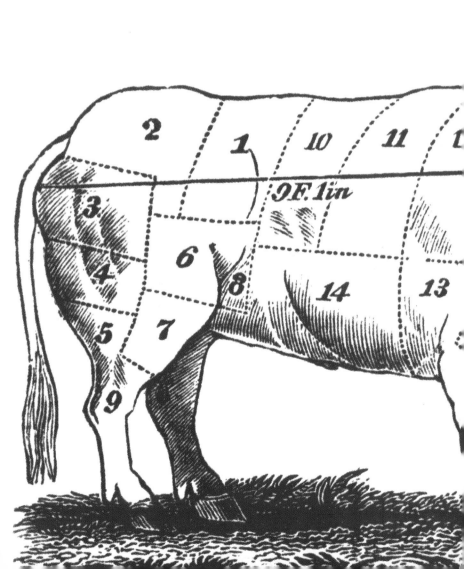

"My daddy, he tickles me.
He says he made me because
he fed me steak when
I was a baby—going without shoes,
he says, to pay the food bill.
How could I
eat steak when
I didn't have
one tooth?
What a lot of bull."

16

18

15

"*I woke up this morning*
feeling good and black.
I got out of my black bed,
I put on my black robe,
I played all my best black records,
and drank some black coffee.
Then I put on my black shoes and
I walked out my black door...

and Oh Lord, white snow!"

"I dig them cats!"

ON ATTENDING ONE OF HIS FIRST
NATION OF ISLAM MEETINGS

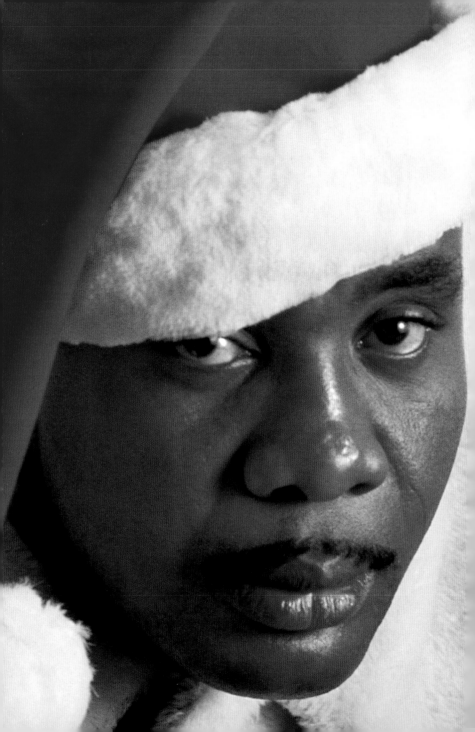

*"Liston is the
last man on earth
you wanna see
come down
your chimney
on Christmas Eve."*

*COMMENTING ON THE
DEPICTION OF SONNY LISTON AS
THE FIRST BLACK SANTA*

ESQUIRE *COVER, DECEMBER 1963,
CREATED BY GEORGE LOIS*

"Free!
I'll fight you free!
You think I'm jiving, Chump?
I'll fight you free, right here!"

TRYING TO GOAD SONNY LISTON INTO
A BARE-KNUCKLE FISTFIGHT
IN THE MIDDLE OF THE DAY IN A LOCAL PARK

*"I could see I was beginning
to get to him a little, but not enough.
Finally, I had to shoot
a loaded water pistol at him."*

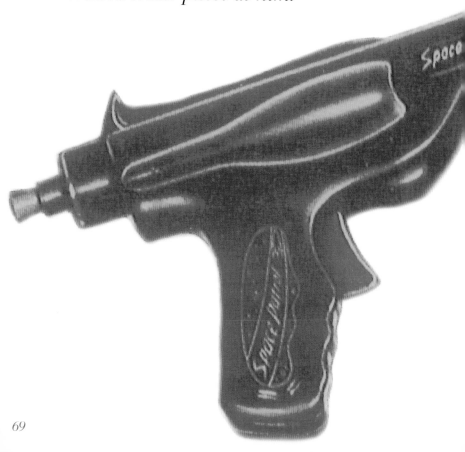

INCITING SONNY LISTON TO FIGHT HIM IN THE RING

*"Liston's a slugger,
and sluggers don't like crazies.
Nobody can ever tell
what a crazy's gonna do next."*

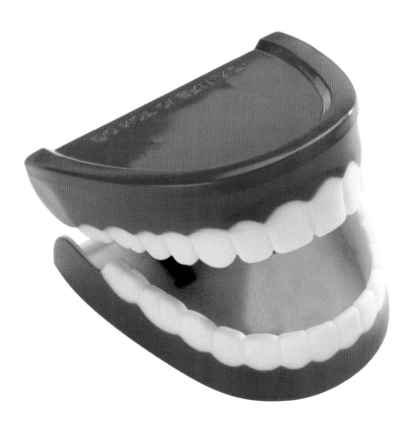

"Yeah, they're getting that Medicare
Ready for that old man,
And when I hit him in the mouth,
He's gonna need DENTIcare."

BEFORE THE FIRST SONNY LISTON FIGHT

"Clay comes out to meet Liston
And Liston starts to retreat
If Liston goes back any further
He'll end up in a ringside seat
Clay swings with a left
Clay swings with a right
Look at young Cassius
Carry the fight
Liston keeps backing
But there's not enough room
It's a matter of time
There, Clay lowers the boom
Now Clay swings with a right
What a beautiful swing

And the punch raises the Bear
Clear out of the ring
Liston is still rising
And the ref wears a frown
For he can't start counting
Till Sonny comes down
Now Liston disappears from view
The crowd is getting frantic
But our radar stations have picked him up
He's somewhere over the Atlantic
Who would have thought
When they came to the fight
That they'd witness the launching
Of a human satellite?...

...Yes, the crowd did not dream
When they laid down their money
That they would see
A total eclipse of the Sonny!"

"**S**onny Liston is great
But he'll fall in eight."

"Fifteen referees.
I want 15 referees to be at this fight...

*...because there ain't no one man who can
keep up with the pace I'm gonna set except me."*

"'Lemme go,'
and I'm telling
them out the side
of my mouth,
'You better NOT
lemme go!'"

*BEING HELD BACK
BY ANGELO DUNDEE
AS HE FEIGNS AN
ATTACK ON A VISITING
SONNY LISTON*

Sonny Liston:
"*Look, Clay, this is for you!*"

AT LISTON'S TRAINING CAMP, DRIVING
A DEVASTATING LEFT HOOK INTO A HEAVY BAG

Cassius Clay:
"*Yeah, but the bag can't
punch back.*"

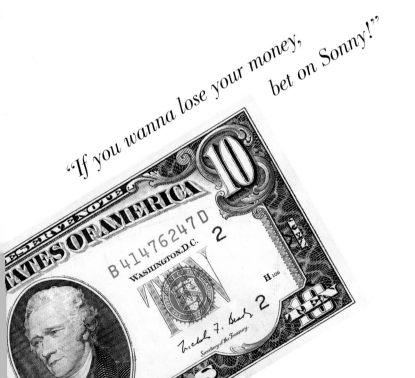

"If you wanna lose your money,
bet on Sonny!"

I am the greatest,
I'm pretty,
I'm pretty,
I'm a baaad man,
You heard me I'm a baaad man,
Archie Moore fell in four,
Liston wanted me more,
So since he's so great,
I'll make him fall in eight,
I'm a baaad man,
I'm King of the World!
I'm 22 years old and ain't
Gotta mark on my face."

*"That's the only time
I was scared in the ring.
Sonny Liston.
First time.
First round.
Said he was gonna kill me."*

"I am the King!
King of the World.
Eat your words!
Eat!
Eat your words!
I am the Greatest!"

THE NEW CHAMPION SCREAMING
AT RINGSIDE REPORTERS AFTER HIS
7TH ROUND TKO OF
SONNY LISTON (MOST RESPECTED
REPORTERS HAD DISMISSED
CLAY AS A LOUDMOUTH AND A FAKE)

A CLARION CALL
CELEBRATING
HIS CHAMPIONSHIP,
AS WELL AS
STRONGLY HINTING
HE HAD BECOME
A MUSLIM

"A rooster crows only when it sees light.
Put him in the dark and he'll never crow.

I have seen the light and I'm crowing."

THE MORNING AFTER BECOMING HEAVYWEIGHT CHAMPION OF THE WORLD

"A certain New York expert who predicted that Sonny Liston would whup me with three punches and a scowl, went to a psychiatrist after the fight. He went for two reasons. First of all, he was in need of mental help."

SIGMUND FREUD,
THE AUSTRIAN PSYCHIATRIST AND
FOUNDER OF PSYCHOANALYSIS

*"Liston felt like he was getting
ready to start off on some
bum-of-the-month club like Joe Louis did.
When he looked at me
all he could see was my big mouth!"*

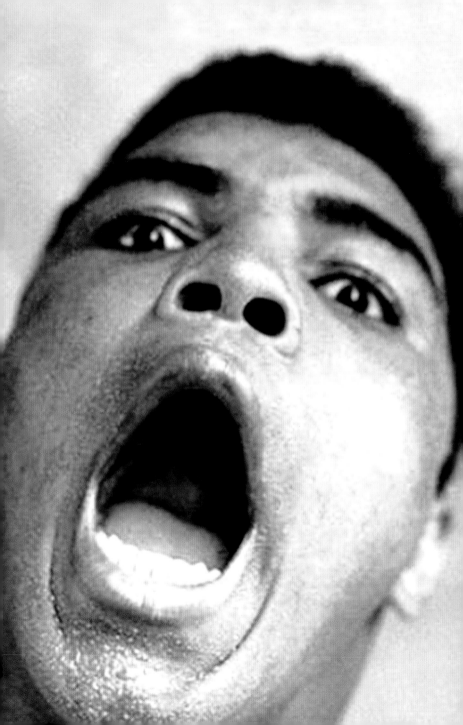

"We shall overcome."

DR. MARTIN LUTHER KING JR.

*"I don't say we shall overcome,
because I done overcome."*

CASSIUS CLAY

*"Do you know what?
Martin Luther King was the only
Negro leader who sent
me a telegram when I became
champion of the world
—the only one."*

PRIVATE
PROPERTY
KEEP OUT

"I'm the People's Champion.
You can walk up to me
and say 'Hello' without paying.
Try getting near to
Frank Sinatra or Elvis.
There are no bodyguards around
THIS camp."

*"Cassius Marcellus Clay.
He was a Kentucky white man who
owned my great-granddaddy and
named my great-granddaddy after him.
And then my granddaddy got named,
and then my daddy, and now it's me.
We were named after our white slavemaster."*

WELL BEFORE THE CIVIL WAR,
SLAVE OWNER CASSIUS MARCELLUS CLAY
REDEEMED HIS LEGACY BY
FREEING HIS SLAVES AND BECOMING AN
ACTIVE ABOLITIONIST, EDITING
AN EMANCIPATIONIST NEWSPAPER–
HE LIVED THE REST OF HIS LIFE
AS A KENTUCKY LEGISLATOR, SOLDIER,
STATESMAN, DIPLOMAT, AND
A DRAMATIC SYMBOL
OF CHRISTIAN REDEMPTION.

"Cassius Clay is my slave name!
Clay means dirt.
I didn't choose it, and I didn't want it.
I am Muhammad Ali, a free name—
Muhammad means 'worthy of praise'
and Ali means 'most high'—
and I insist people use it when speaking
to me and of me."

"In 1960, when I was a nobody, Dick Schaap saw me off at Idlewild Airport in New York on my way to Rome to fight in the Olympics. Four years later, the airport and me changed our names."

"I don't have to be...

what you want me to be."

*"Elijah is not teaching hate
when he tells us about all the evil things
the white man has done,
any more than you are teaching hate
when you tell about what
Hitler did to the Jews.
That's not hate, that's history."*

"People change their
names all the time,
and no one complains.
Actors and actresses
change their names.
The pope
changes his name.
Sugar Ray Robinson
and Joe Louis
changed
their names."

Alphonso D'Abruzzo
Allen Königsberg
Frederick Austerlitz
Benjamin Kubelsky
Charles Buchinski
Melvin Kaminsky
Howard Cohen
Bernard Schwartz
Doris von Kappelhoff
Issur Danielovitch Demsky
Frances Gumm
Archibald Leach
William Beedle Jr.
Eleanora Fagan
Giovanni Battista Montini
Rose Hovick
Joseph Louis Barrow
Norma Jeane Baker
Walker Smith Jr.
Richard Starkey
Samuel Clemens
Cassius Marcellus Clay Jr.

Alan Alda
Woody Allen
Fred Astaire
Jack Benny
Charles Bronson
Mel Brooks
Howard Cosell
Tony Curtis
Doris Day
Kirk Douglas
Judy Garland
Cary Grant
William Holden
Billie Holiday
Pope Paul VI
Gypsy Rose Lee
Joe Louis
Marilyn Monroe
Sugar Ray Robinson
Ringo Starr
Mark Twain
Muhammad Ali

"I am America.
I am the past you won't recognize;
but get used to me.
Black, confident, cocky–
My name, not yours.
My religion, not yours.
My goal, my own.
Get used to me."

"What is all the commotion about?
Nobody asks other boxers about their religion.
But now that I'm the champion,
I am the king, so it seems the world is all
shook up about what I believe.
You call it the Black Muslims, I don't.
This is the name that has
been given to us by the press.
The real name is Islam.
That means peace."

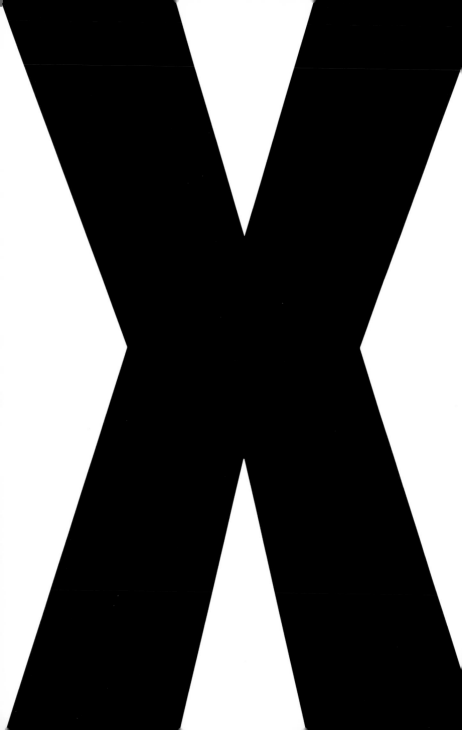

*"I was forced to make a choice
when Elijah Muhammad insisted
I break with Malcolm.
Turning my back on Malcolm
was one of the mistakes
that I regret most in my life.
I wish I had been able
to tell Malcolm I was sorry,
that he was right about
so many things. But he was killed
before I got the chance."*

"*I hated every minute of training,
but I said, 'Don't quit.
Suffer now and live the rest of your life
as a champion.'*"

"**I** outwit them
And then outhit them."

*"All types of women—white women, too—make passes at me.
A black man should be killed if he's messing with a white woman."*

IN 1964 ALI TURNED DOWN PLAYING
JACK JOHNSON IN A MOVIE ROLE BECAUSE
THE PART WOULD HAVE FORCED HIM
TO BE PORTRAYED MARRYING A WHITE WOMAN

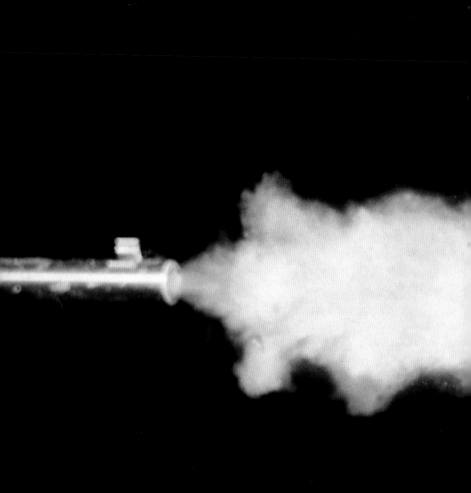

"*Allah will protect me.*
Besides, I'm too fast to be hit by a bullet."

AFTER RECEIVING NUMEROUS DEATH THREATS
BEFORE THE SECOND LISTON FIGHT,
ALI TURNED DOWN POLICE PROTECTION.

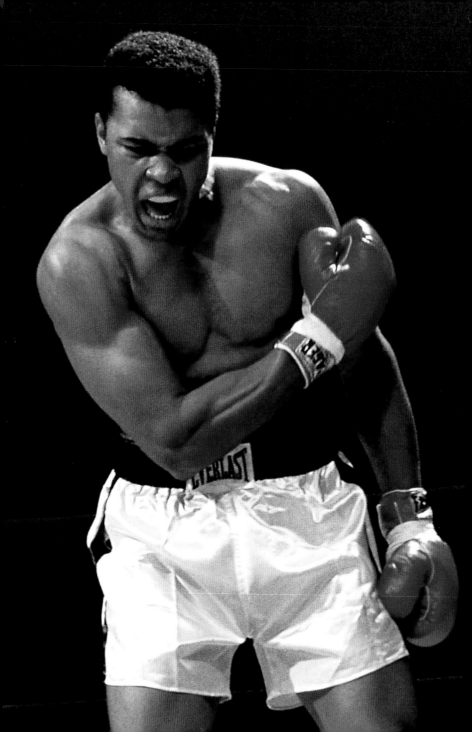

"Get up and fight, sucka!
Get up and fight, you bum!
You're supposed to be so bad!
Nobody will believe this!"

ALI SCREAMING OVER THE KO'd LISTON
IN THEIR SECOND FIGHT
(LISTON HAD BEEN A FIVE-TO-ONE FAVORITE
TO WIN HIS TITLE BACK,
DESPITE HIS CRUSHING DEFEAT
A YEAR EARLIER)

THE CONCORD MINUTE MAN,
BY DANIEL CHESTER FRENCH,
COMMEMORATING THE
"SHOT HEARD 'ROUND THE WORLD,"
THE FIRST BATTLE AGAINST THE
BRITISH THAT IGNITED THE
AMERICAN REVOLUTIONARY WAR.
(THE BRONZE USED WAS
MELTED-DOWN CIVIL WAR
CANNONS)

"Just call me the Minute Man."

AFTER BEING TOLD THAT HIS 1:49 VICTORY
OVER SONNY LISTON HAD BEEN
OFFICIALLY RULED A ONE-MINUTE KO
(IT HAD TAKEN LONGER TO SING THE NATIONAL ANTHEM)

"Champs don't take out garbage."

ALI'S REPLY TO HIS (FIRST) WIFE SONJI'S REQUEST

"Hello? City Morgue!"

ANSWERING A RINGING TELEPHONE
AT THE MIAMI BEACH FIFTH STREET GYM

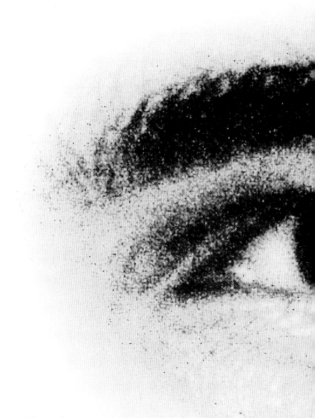

*"I'm color-blind.
I love people.
Black, white, rich or poor."*

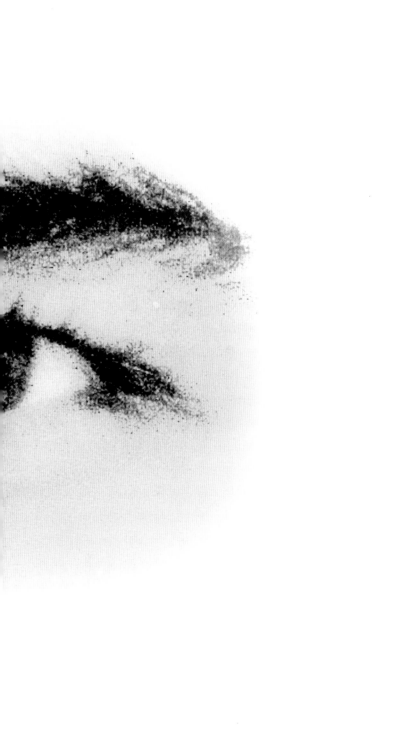

"*People keep asking me
what would happen if I fought
Wilt Chamberlain.
You know what would happen?
TIM-BERRRRR!*"

*SPEAKING ABOUT THE SEVEN-FOOT-ONE
BASKETBALL SUPERSTAR*

"*I started out making $4 for my first fight. But imagine paying $25,000 for a painting...look at me! White people gonna pay $25,000 for my picture!*"

*"People don't realize 'til it's gone.
Like President Kennedy—nobody like him.
Like the Beatles, there will never
be anything like them."*

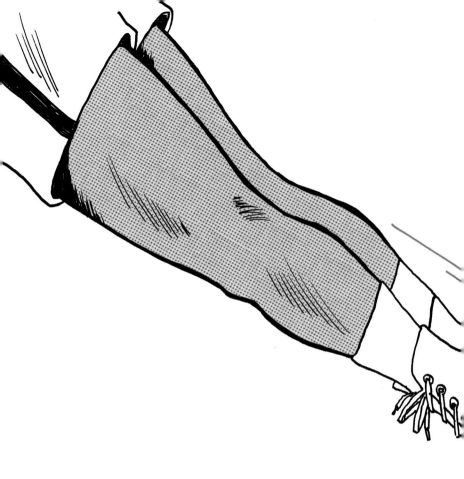

Stewardess:
"Buckle up, Mr. Ali."

Muhammad Ali:
"Superman don't need no seatbelt."

Stewardess:
"Superman don't need no airplane, either."

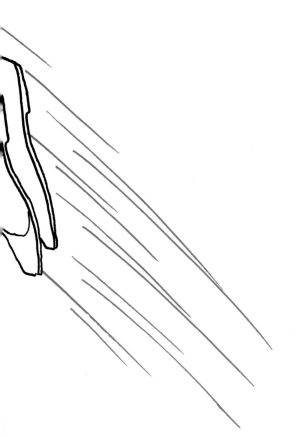

*"No one knows
what to say in the loser's
locker room."*

"I called my training camp Fighter's Heaven."

ALI'S TRAINING CAMP IN DEER LAKE, PENNSYLVANIA, WHERE GIANT BOULDERS (SIX FEET LONG AND FOUR FEET HIGH), WERE STREWN AROUND THE PROPERTY, AND HAND-PAINTED BY CASSIUS CLAY SR. WITH THE NAMES OF PREVIOUS GREAT CHAMPIONS:

JACK DEMPSEY
KID GAVILAN
JACK JOHNSON
SONNY LISTON
JOE LOUIS
ROCKY MARCIANO
ARCHIE MOORE
SUGAR RAY ROBINSON
JERSEY JOE WALCOTT

Rules of M

1 PLEASE TO KEEP OUTE. exce
2 COOKE. shall designate pot scourer
   supreme AUTHORITY AT ALL
3 NO REMARKS AT ALL WILL BE
   the weakness of soupe or the st
4 What goes in stews & soups is
5 If you MUST stioke your finger in
6 DONT CRITICIZE the coffee you n
7 ANYONE bringinge guestes in for
   on skull with sharpe object.
8 PLEASE WAITE Rome wasn't burr
9 IF YOU MUST pinche somethinge ir
10 this is my kitchen if you don't b

"My daddy was a poet, But he didn't know it."

SIGN IN AUNT CORETTA'S KITCHEN AT HIS
DEER LAKE TRAINING CAMP,
HAND-PAINTED BY ALI'S FATHER,
CASSIUS CLAY SR.

YTCHEN

ress permission of cooke

rs peelers scrapers and **COOKE** has

ED concerning the blackening of toast
the garlic stewe.
dam business.
stick it in the garbage disposal.
e and weak yourself someday.
ut **PRIOR NOTICE** will be awarded thwacks

and it takes awhile to burne the ROASTE.
HEN PINCHIE the **COOKE**!
START SOMETHING.

111

*"How tall are you?
So I can know in advance
how far to step back
when you fall down!"*

ALI'S FAVORITE PUNCH LINE AT
PREFIGHT WEIGH-INS

"I'm gonna put him flat on his back
So that he will start acting black
Because when he was champ
He didn't do as he should
He tried to force himself
Into an all-white neighborhood."

AFTER FLOYD PATTERSON SAID HE WAS
GOING TO BRING THE HEAVYWEIGHT TITLE
"BACK TO AMERICA" BY DEFEATING
MUHAMMAD ALI, IMPLYING THAT A MUSLIM
COULD NOT BE AN AMERICAN

"Catching flies is better training than hitting the speedbag."

EIGHT FLIES CAUGHT AND KILLED,
MIDAIR, BY THE HAND OF
MUHAMMAD ALI IN THE COURSE
OF A 15-MINUTE INTERVIEW

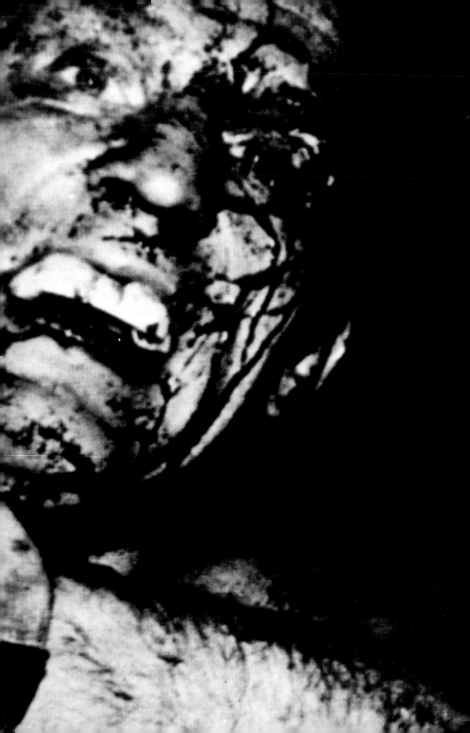

*"I can't stand the sight of blood.
In many of my fights I had to look away."*

*THE COURAGEOUS BRIT HENRY COOPER
TOOK A TERRIBLE BEATING
FROM ALI UNTIL HE WAS KO'd IN ROUND SIX.*

"Rivers, ponds, lakes and streams—
they all have different names,
but they all contain water.
Just as religions do—they all contain truths."

*"I love Westerns.
That's why I went to see
Midnight Cowboy.
I thought it was going
to be a Western."*

DUSTIN HOFFMAN
AS RATSO RIZZO
IN MIDNIGHT COWBOY

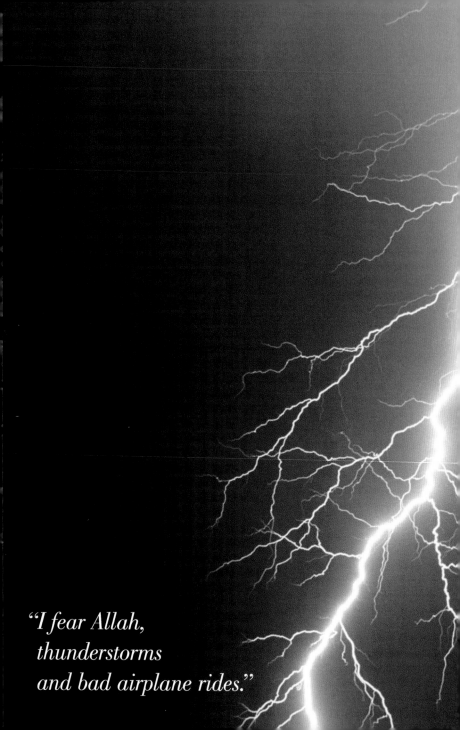

"I fear Allah,
 thunderstorms
 and bad airplane rides."

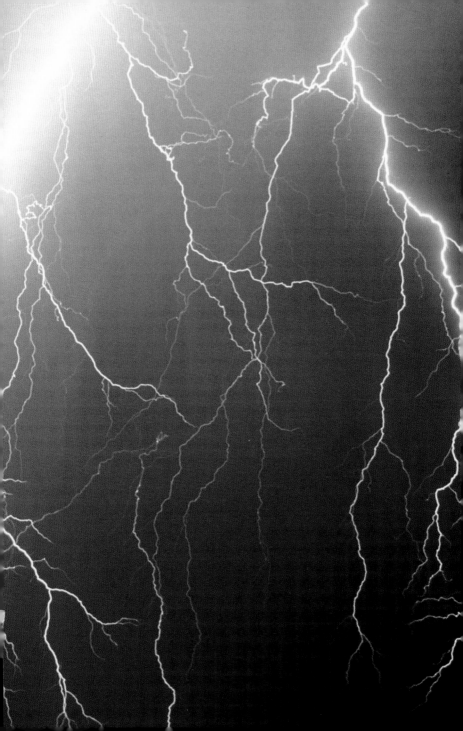

"It's just a job.
Grass grows.
Birds fly.
Waves pound the sand.
I beat people up."

*"I don't call it fear,
I call it being scared to death!"*

*IN ANSWER TO A SPORT MAGAZINE INTERVIEWER
ASKING IF FEAR IS WHAT KEEPS HIM ALERT*

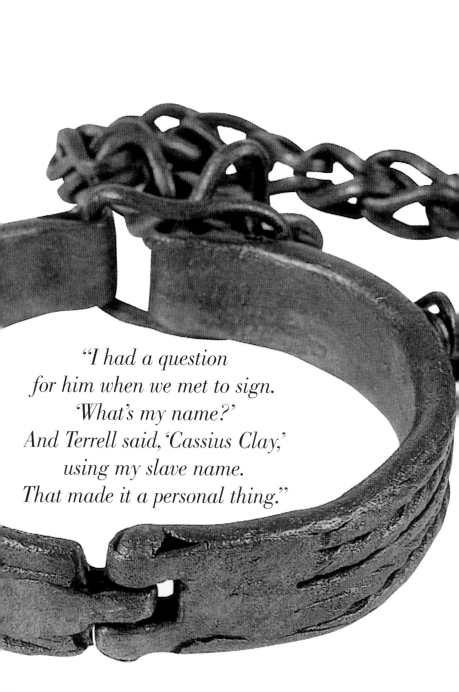

"*I had a question
for him when we met to sign.
'What's my name?'
And Terrell said,'Cassius Clay,'
using my slave name.
That made it a personal thing.*"

"*What's my name, Uncle Tom?*
What's my name, fool?
Don't you fall, Uncle Tom.
Don't you fall."

TAUNTING ERNIE TERRELL IN THE RING
FOR HIS REFUSING TO ACKNOWLEDGE
MUHAMMAD ALI'S NEW NAME

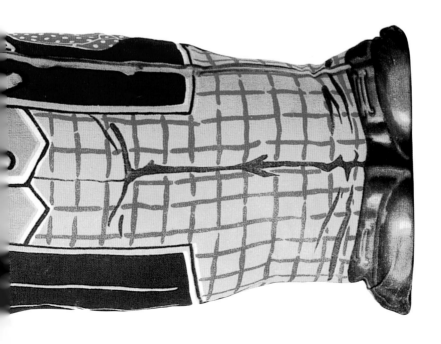

"This is the legend of Muhammad Ali,
The greatest fighter that ever will be.
He talks a great deal and brags, indeed,
Of a powerful punch and blinding speed.
Ali's got a left, Ali's got a right,
If he hits you once, you're asleep for the night.

ZZZZZ

ZZZZZ

"*I should be a postage stamp.
That's the only way
I'll ever get licked.*"

*"No pork,
soda pop,
cigarettes,
alcohol–
ever!"*

*"Beating me
is like beating Joe Louis
or being the man
who shot Jesse James."*

"I don't always know what I"

lking about but I know I'm right."

MUHAMMAD ALI ON HIS GOLF GAME:

"I'm the best. I just haven't played yet."

Ali: *"Y'know, I got the fastest left hand in the history of boxing."*

Lois: *"Wel-l-l, sure...the fastest* heavyweight.*"*

Ali: *"No, no, no. The fastest ever–of all time!"*

Lois: *"Gee, Champ, I could name a bunch of middleweights and lightweights who were quicker. Sugar Ray Robinson, Willie Pep..."*

Ali: *"No, no, I am the fastest in ring history! Wanna see it?"*

Lois: *"Well, er..."*

(WITHOUT MOVING A MUSCLE)

Ali: *"Wanna see it again?!"*

"**I**'ve got speed, power and endurance
And anyone who fights me
Had better take out extra life insurance."

The
Prudential

"*We know that every white ain't devil-hearted, and we got black people who are devils— the worst devils I've run into can be my own kind.*"

*"Howard Hughes dies,
with all his billions, not a tear.
Joe Louis, everybody cried."*

*"The masters got two of us big ol'
black slaves and let us
fight it out while they bet:*

'My slave can beat your slave.'
That's what I see when
I see two black people fighting!'"

TO BE SOLD & LET

BY PUBLIC AUCTION,

On *MONDAY the 18th of MAY. 1829,*

UNDER THE TREES.

FOR SALE,
THE THREE FOLLOWING

SLAVES,

viz.

HANNIBAL, about 30 Years old, an excellent House Servant, of Good Character.
WILLIAM, about 35 Years old, a Labourer.
NANCY, an excellent House Servant and Nurse,

The MEN belonging to "LEECH'S" Estate, and the WOMAN to Mrs. D. SMIT

TO BE LET,

On the usual conditions of the Hirer finding them in Food, Clot ing, and Medical ance,

THE FOLLOWING

MALE and FEMALE

SLAVES,

OF GOOD CHARACTERS.

ROBERT BAGLEY, about 20 Years old, a good House Servant.
WILLIAM BAGLEY, about 18 Years old, a Labourer.
JOHN ARMS, about 18 Years old.
JACK ANTONIA, about 40 Years old, a Labourer.
PHILIP, an Excellent Fisherman.
HARRY, about 27 Years old, a good House Servant.
LUCY, a Young Woman of good Character, used to House Work and the Nursery.
ELIZA, an Excellent Washerwoman.
CLARA, an Excellent Washerwoman.
FANNY, about 14 Years old, House Servant.
SARAH, about 14 Years old. House Servant.

Also for Sale, at Eleven o'Clock,

Fine Rice, Gram, Paddy, Books, Muslins, Needles, Pins, Ribbons, &c. &c.

AT ONE O'CLOCK, THAT CELEBRATED ENGLISH HORSE

BLUCHER,

ADDISON PRINTER GOVERNMENT OFFICE.

131

"*Those ads on selling slaves should be in every history book in our schools, so everybody can see that we were treated no better than animals.*"

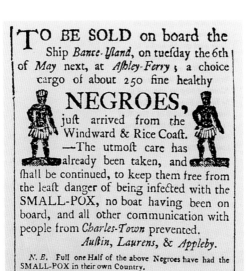

TO BE SOLD on board the Ship *Bance-Island*, on tuesday the 6th of *May* next, at *Ashley-Ferry*; a choice cargo of about 250 fine healthy NEGROES, just arrived from the Windward & Rice Coast. —The utmost care has already been taken, and shall be continued, to keep them free from the least danger of being infected with the SMALL-POX, no boat having been on board, and all other communication with people from *Charles-Town* prevented.

Austin, Laurens, & Appleby.

N. B. Full one Half of the above Negroes have had the SMALL-POX in their own Country.

"I said I was the greatest...

...not the smartest."

*AFTER FAILING
THE WRITTEN EXAM AT THE
ARMY INDUCTION CENTER*

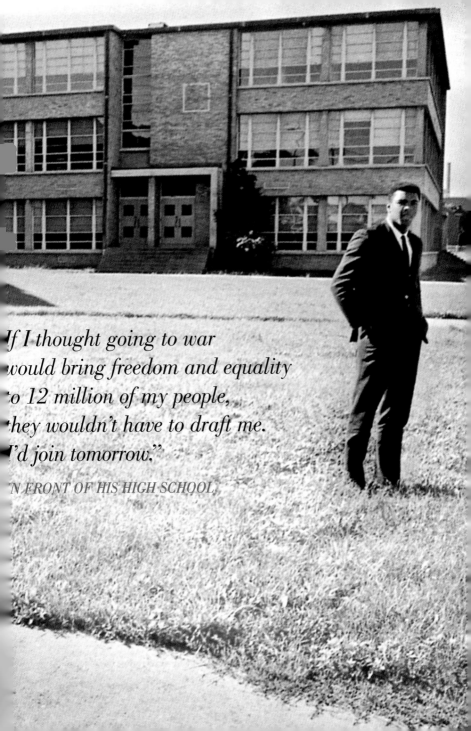

"If I thought going to war
would bring freedom and equality
to 12 million of my people,
they wouldn't have to draft me.
I'd join tomorrow."

IN FRONT OF HIS HIGH SCHOOL,

"I have nothing to lose by standing up and following my beliefs.

We've been in jail for 400 years."

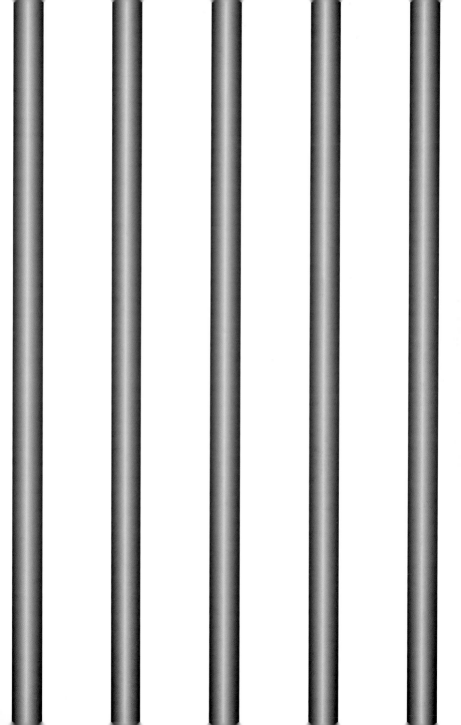

"Hell no, I ain't gonna go
On the war in Vietnam I sing this song
I ain't got no quarrel with them Viet Cong
Clean out my cell
And take my tail to jail
Without bail
'Cause better to be in jail fed
Than to be in Vietnam, dead"

"You want me to do what the white man says,
and go fight a war against some people
I don't know nothing about—get some freedom
for some other people when my own people
can't get theirs here?
You want me to be so scared of the white man
I'll go and get two arms shot off and
ten medals so you can give me a small salary
and pat my head and say,
'Good boy, he fought for his country.'
Every day they die in Vietnam for nothing."

PROPORTIONATELY, MORE BLACK SOLDIERS
DIED IN VIETNAM THAN OTHER RACES:
29% WHO DIED WERE BLACK, EVEN THOUGH
BLACKS MADE UP ONLY 11% OF THE
U.S. POPULATION

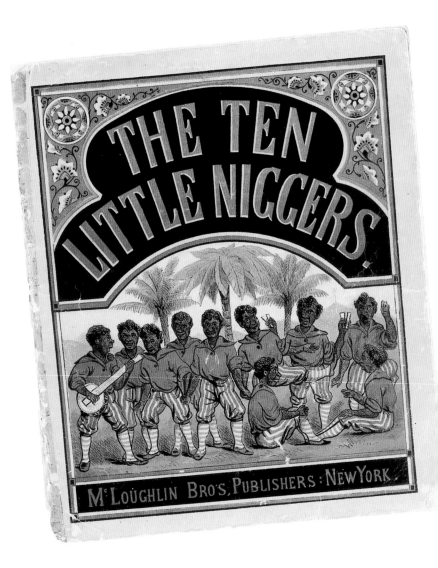

THE TEN LITTLE NIGGERS.

McLoughlin Bro's. Publishers : New York.

"No Vietnamese ever called me 'Nigger.'"

*"I see signs saying
'LBJ, how many kids did you kill today?'
I didn't write that. I didn't say that.
I didn't say nothin' half that bad!
White American kids are sayin' that!"*

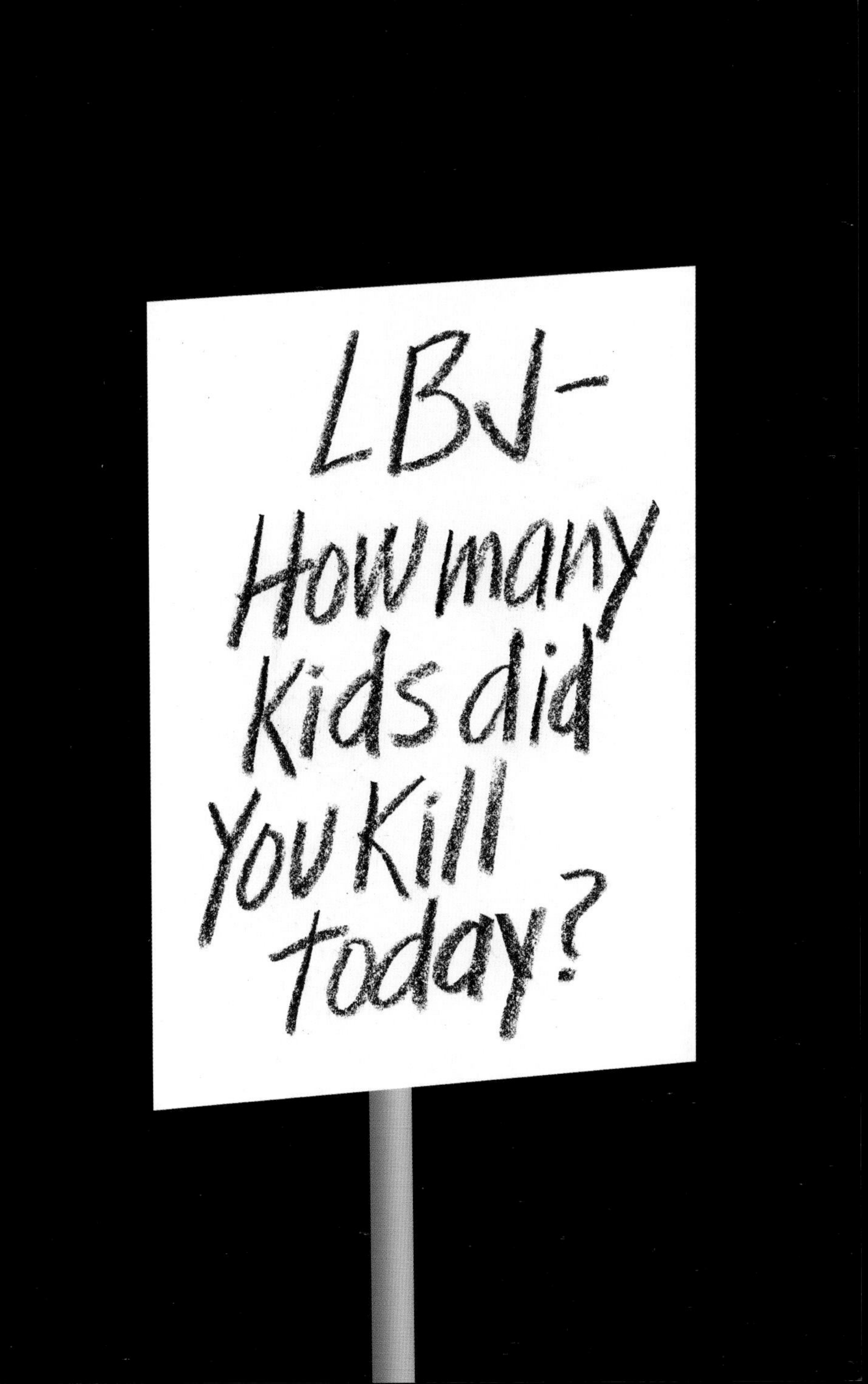
LBJ -
How many
kids did
You Kill
today?

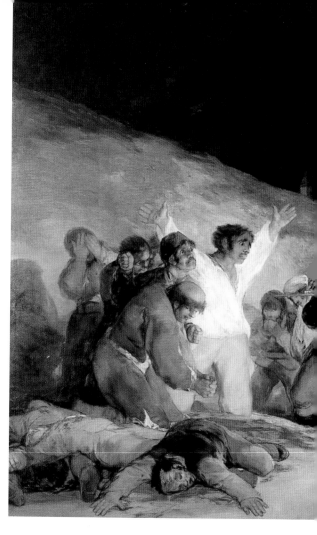

THE GREAT PAINTING BY FRANCISCO DE GOYA,
THE THIRD OF MAY 1808,
COMMEMORATES THE SPANISH RESISTANCE
AGAINST THE INVADING NAPOLEON.

"Whatever the punishment,
whatever the persecution is for standing up
for my religious beliefs–
even if it means facing a firing squad–
I'll face it. I'm ready to die."

*"Why should they ask me
to put on a uniform
and go 10,000 miles from
home and drop bombs
and bullets on brown people
in Vietnam while
so-called Negro people in Louisville
are treated like dogs."*

"I try to think of myself as a WHITE President,
ready at least to be fair to the black people
of America. I'd say 'We white Americans are
guilty of many crimes. The worst crime
our ancestors committed was when they brought
those slaves over from Africa. But first
I'm gonna stop that war in Vietnam tomorrow.
I'm going to take $25 billion I was gonna
spend on helicopters for Vietnam and it's gonna
go to Alabama and Georgia and Mississippi
and pay for $25 billion worth of houses,
nice brick houses with at least three bedrooms
in each one. Each black family
who needs it is going to be given a home!'"

Mama Bird:
"G.G., do the right thing.
If I were you, I would go ahead
and take the step.
If I were you I would join the Army.
Do you understand me, son?"

Muhammad:
"Mama, I love you. Whatever I do,
Mama, remember I love you."

ODESSA CLAY ON A PHONE CALL TO HER SON THE DAY
BEFORE HE WOULD BE ORDERED, ONE LAST TIME,
TO STEP FORWARD AT AN INDUCTION CENTER TO ENTER
THE ARMY OR FACE IMPRISONMENT

PIETÀ (1499 A.D.), MICHELANGELO'S
SYMBOLIC AND TIMELESS MASTERPIECE
REPRESENTING A MOTHER'S LOVE
AND PROFOUND RECOGNITION OF HER
SON'S DIVINE SACRIFICE

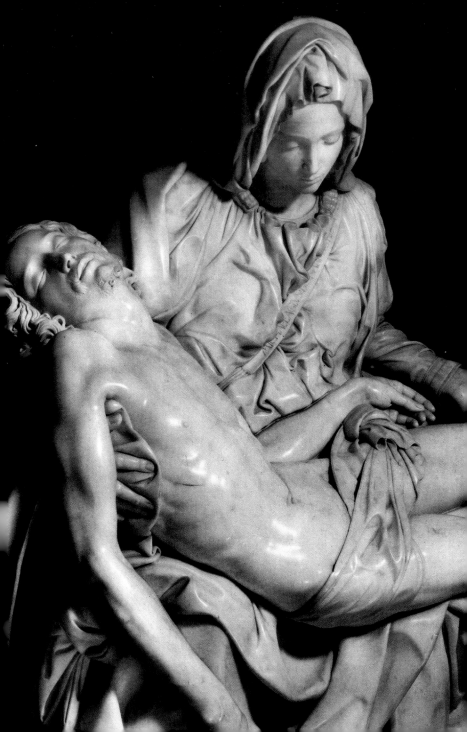

*"Every man wonders
what he is going to do when he is
put on the chopping block,
when he's going to be tested."*

EVENTUALLY, ALI'S COURAGE FORCED
DR. MARTIN LUTHER KING TO BREAK HIS
SILENCE ON THE VIETNAM WAR WITH
THIS DEFENSE OF THE HEAVYWEIGHT CHAMPION:
"HE IS GIVING UP MILLIONS OF DOLLARS
IN ORDER TO STAND UP FOR WHAT
HIS CONSCIENCE TELLS HIM IS RIGHT.
EVERY YOUNG MAN IN THIS COUNTRY WHO
BELIEVES THIS WAR IS ABOMINABLE
AND UNJUST SHOULD FILE
TO BE A CONSCIENTIOUS OBJECTOR."

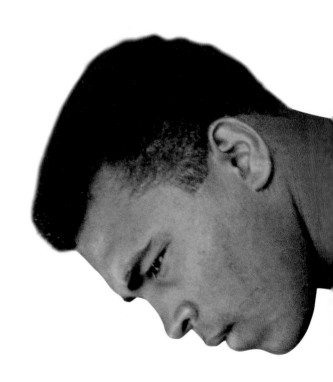

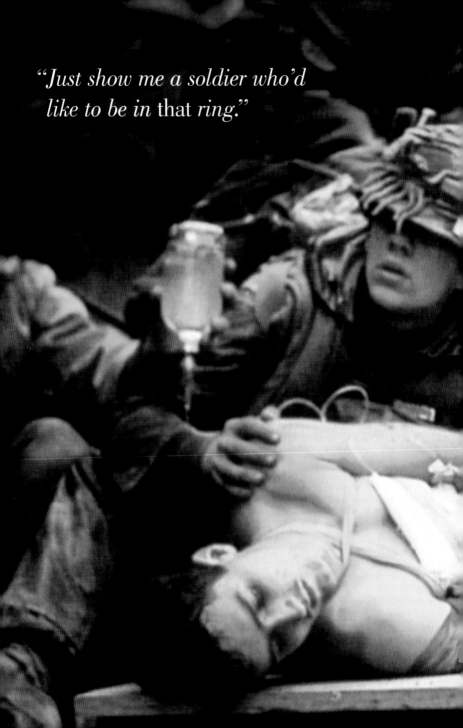

"*Just show me a soldier who'd like to be in that ring.*"

"GOD DON'T WANT ME TO GO DOWN

FOR STANDING UP!"

"*America is my birth country.
They make the rules,
and if they want to put me in jail,
I'll go to jail.
But I'm an American and
I'm not running away.*"

*IN ANSWER TO WHETHER HE WOULD FLEE
THE DRAFT BY STAYING IN CANADA AFTER THE
GEORGE CHUVALO FIGHT IN TORONTO
(ALI DEFENDED HIS TITLE FOUR TIMES OVERSEAS
BECAUSE HE WAS UNWELCOME IN HIS
OWN COUNTRY)*

"*I grew to love
the Jack Johnson image.
I wanted to be rough,
tough, arrogant,
the nigger white folks
didn't like.*"

"*History all over again!*"

*REFERRING TO JACK JOHNSON,
AFTER ALI WAS EXILED FROM THE RING
FOR REFUSING THE DRAFT–
FOR THE SECOND TIME, A BLACK
HEAVYWEIGHT CHAMPION
HAD STOOD UP TO WHITE AMERICA*

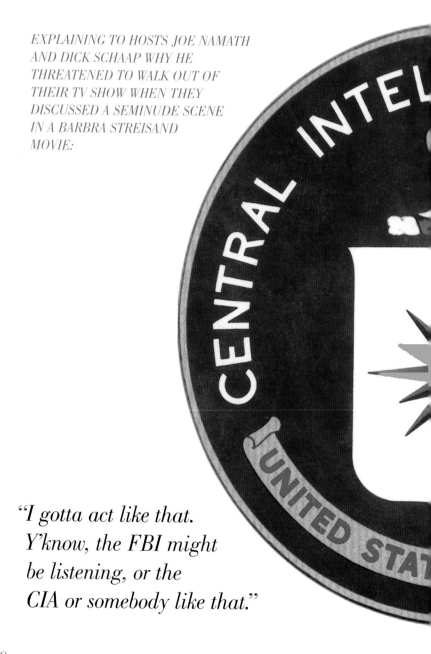

EXPLAINING TO HOSTS JOE NAMATH AND DICK SCHAAP WHY HE THREATENED TO WALK OUT OF THEIR TV SHOW WHEN THEY DISCUSSED A SEMINUDE SCENE IN A BARBRA STREISAND MOVIE:

"*I gotta act like that. Y'know, the FBI might be listening, or the CIA or somebody like that.*"

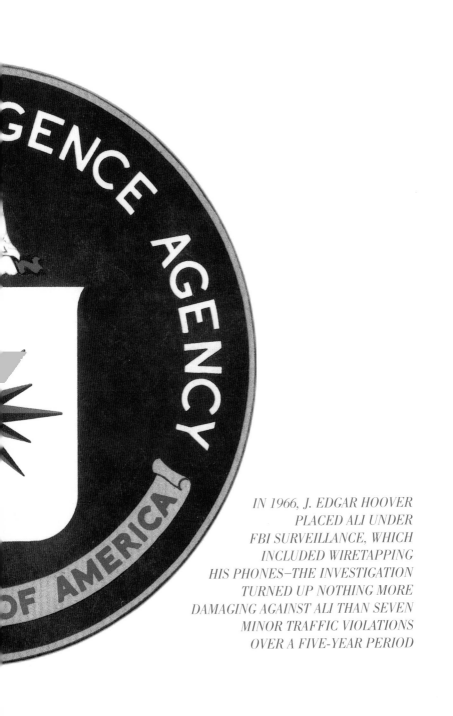

IN 1966, J. EDGAR HOOVER
PLACED ALI UNDER
FBI SURVEILLANCE, WHICH
INCLUDED WIRETAPPING
HIS PHONES—THE INVESTIGATION
TURNED UP NOTHING MORE
DAMAGING AGAINST ALI THAN SEVEN
MINOR TRAFFIC VIOLATIONS
OVER A FIVE-YEAR PERIOD

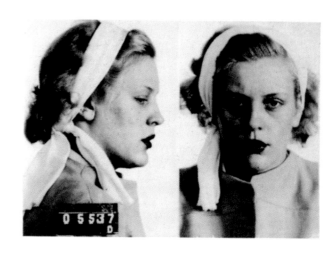

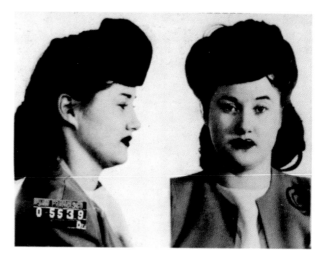

*WHEN ALI SOUGHT A COMEBACK FIGHT IN 1968,
NEVADA WAS CONTROLLED BY THE MOB
AND RIGHT-WING BILLIONAIRE HOWARD HUGHES.
HUGHES (WHO HAD STRONG POLITICAL
CONNECTIONS WITH RICHARD NIXON) CONSIDERED
ALI AN "UNDESIRABLE," UNSUITED TO
FIGHT IN LAS VEGAS—THE AMERICAN CAPITAL OF
GAMBLING, PROSTITUTION AND VICE.*

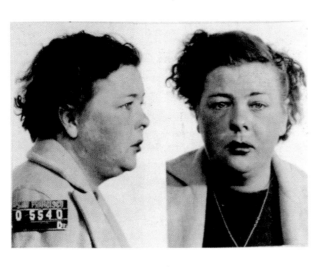

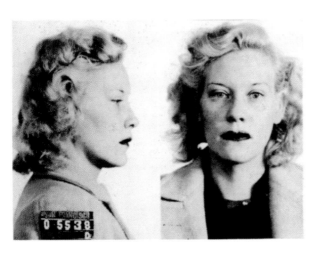

"Me, corrupt Las Vegas?!"

*"I was determined
to be one nigger
that the white man
didn't get...
you understand?
One nigger
you ain't gonna get."*

"Thanks for being in my corner, Floyd."

AFTER FLOYD PATTERSON TAUNTED ALI ON HIS
CONVERSION TO ISLAM, ALI HUMILIATED
PATTERSON IN THEIR 1965 CHAMPIONSHIP BOUT.
EIGHT MONTHS LATER, GEORGE LOIS
CONVINCED A GRACIOUS FLOYD PATTERSON TO
SPEAK OUT, ON THE COVER OF ESQUIRE,
IN DEFENSE OF ALI'S REFUSAL TO BE INDUCTED
INTO THE ARMY BECAUSE OF HIS
RELIGIOUS BELIEFS. (ALI KEPT HIS MOUTH SHUT
DURING THE ENTIRE SHOOT.)

*"There used to be signs on
Miami Beach that said:
'No Jews or Negroes Allowed.'
Y'know what the Jews did?
They got mad and bought the beach."*

SAINT SEBASTIAN,
BY FRANCESCO BOTTICINI, 1465 A.D.

"Hey, George,
this cat's a Christian!"

*ALI, REALIZING THAT THE POSE
HE WAS TO EMULATE
WAS THAT OF SAINT SEBASTIAN.
LOIS BLURTED BACK,
"HOLY MOSES, YOU'RE RIGHT, CHAMP!"
FINALLY A CALL WAS MADE
TO ELIJAH MUHAMMAD TO OBTAIN
HIS PERMISSION FOR ALI
TO BE DEPICTED AS A CHRISTIAN
PORTRAYAL OF MARTYRDOM.*

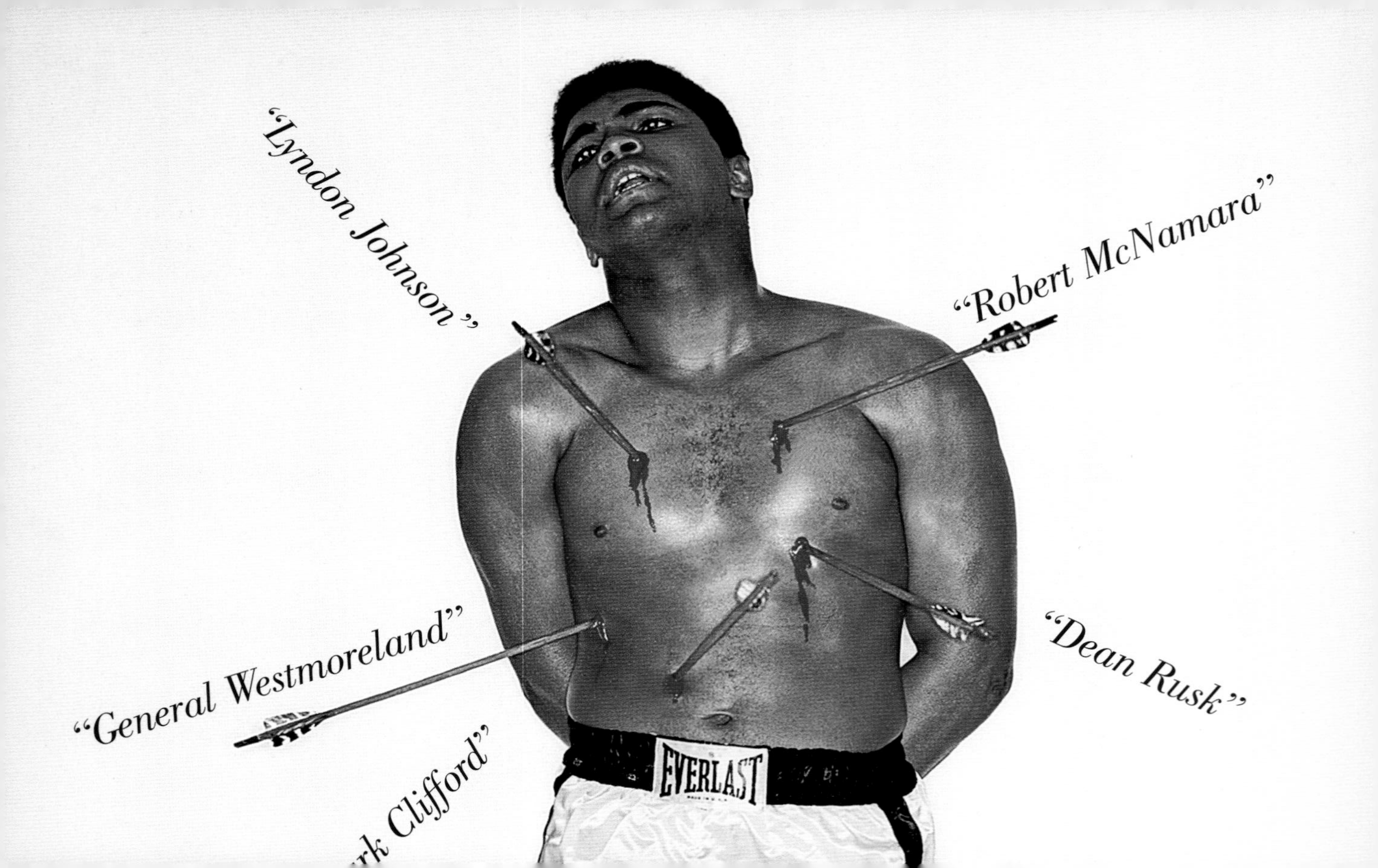

"Robert McNamara"

"Dean Rusk"

"Lyndon Johnson"

"General Westmoreland"

"Clark Clifford"

EVERLAST

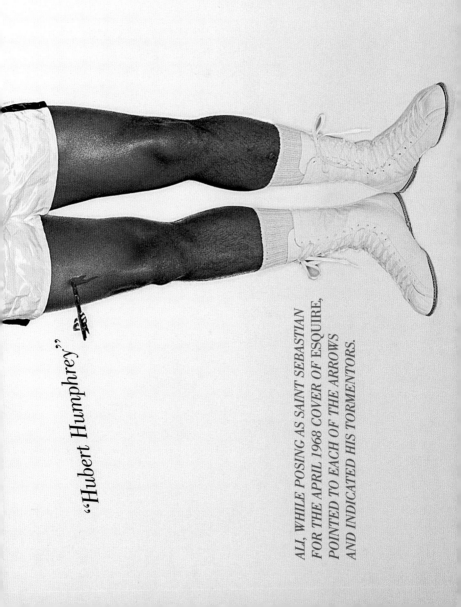

"Hubert Humphrey"

ALI, WHILE POSING AS SAINT SEBASTIAN
FOR THE APRIL 1968 COVER OF ESQUIRE,
POINTED TO EACH OF THE ARROWS
AND INDICATED HIS TORMENTORS.

"I appreciate those 12 good men who stood up for me in the ring on that Esquire *cover. Two blacks and ten whites, and a whole bunch of names inside. It takes a lot of courage to support America's Public Enemy No.1 these days."*

12 ANGRY MEN ENLISTED BY GEORGE LOIS FOR A 1969 ESQUIRE *COVER (WITH ANOTHER 90 LISTED INSIDE)*

1. *RICHARD BENJAMIN*
2. *THEODORE BIKEL*
3. *TRUMAN CAPOTE*
4. *HOWARD COSELL*
5. *SENATOR ERNEST GRUENING*
6. *MICHAEL HARRINGTON*
7. *JAMES EARL JONES*
8. *ROY LICHTENSTEIN*
9. *SIDNEY LUMET*
10. *GEORGE PLIMPTON*
11. *BUDD SCHULBERG*
12. *JOSÉ TORRES*

(KAREEM ABDUL-JABBAR, WHO HAD ONCE BEEN A VISIBLE SUPPORTER OF ALI, WAS A NO-SHOW)

*"They're all afraid of me because
I speak the truth that can set men free."*

*DEPRIVED OF HIS LIVELIHOOD AND AWAITING
THE FINAL JUDGEMENT OF THE COURTS REGARDING
HIS DRAFT-EVASION CONVICTION, MUHAMMAD ALI
BECAME A POLITICAL AND SOCIAL FORCE,
SPEAKING ON COLLEGE CAMPUSES ALL OVER AMERICA.*

"*Ladies and gentlemen, y'know,*
a long time ago when I was a little boy,
I used to throw rocks at a donkey.
And my grandma would say 'Cassius,
quit throwing rocks at that donkey,
'cause someday that donkey gonna die
and come back and haunt you!'
Ladies and gentlemen, I know my
grandma was right, because
I believe that ass is here tonight!'"

A RETORT TO A HECKLER IN
A COLLEGE AUDIENCE WHO HAD SHOUTED
"NIGGER DRAFT-DODGER"

*"There were people who
thought the war
in Vietnam was right.
And those people,
if they went to war, acted
as brave as I did."*

"You done rolled the dice on me.
Now we're going to have to finish the game.
You can't cop out now.
We done gone too far to turn around.
You've got to go on and
either free me or put me in jail,
because I'm going to go on just like
I am, taking my stand.
If I have to go to jail, if I have to die,
I'm ready...
I'm a Freedom Fighter now."

AWAITING THE DECISION OF THE SUPREME COURT

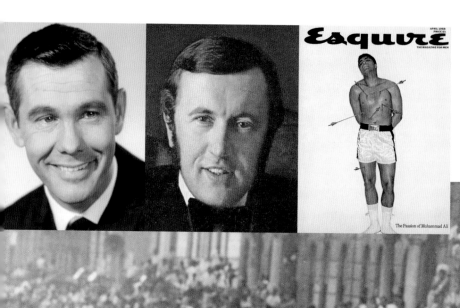

Esquire

APRIL 1968
PRICE $1

THE MAGAZINE FOR MEN

The Passion of Muhammad Ali

"Most people in America, black and white, are fair-minded. Regardless of my religion or the draft, the masses of people have come to my defense: Johnny Carson, David Frost, Esquire, Merv Griffin, the everyday man on the street. The people stood up for me."

"Joe, the whole world wants to know who's the best between you and me. How can they stop what the world wants?"

MUHAMMAD ALI TO JOE FRAZIER

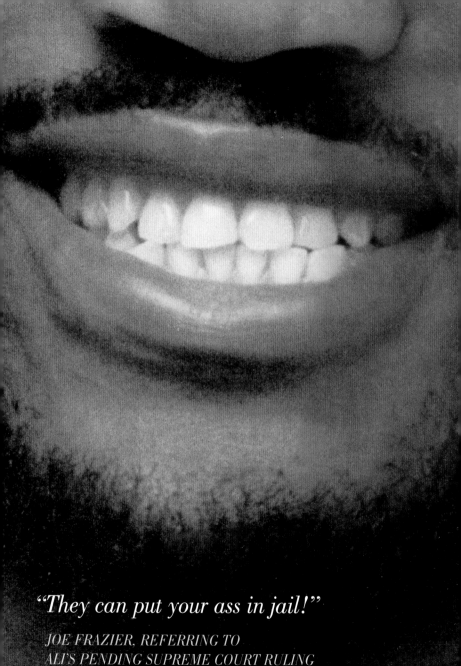

"They can put your ass in jail!"

*JOE FRAZIER, REFERRING TO
ALI'S PENDING SUPREME COURT RULING*

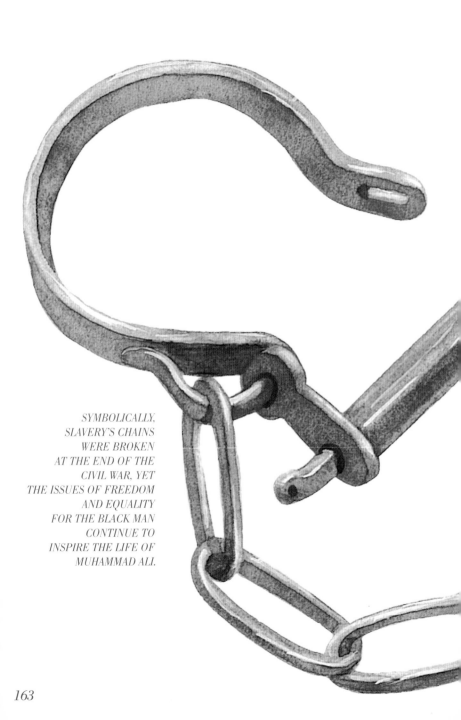

SYMBOLICALLY,
SLAVERY'S CHAINS
WERE BROKEN
AT THE END OF THE
CIVIL WAR, YET
THE ISSUES OF FREEDOM
AND EQUALITY
FOR THE BLACK MAN
CONTINUE TO
INSPIRE THE LIFE OF
MUHAMMAD ALI.

ON JUNE 28, 1971, ALI (CONVINCED HE WOULD BE
GOING TO PRISON) HEARD ON THE RADIO
THAT THE SUPREME COURT HAD UNANIMOUSLY
FREED HIM:

*"It's like a man's been in chains
all his life and suddenly
the chains are taken off."*

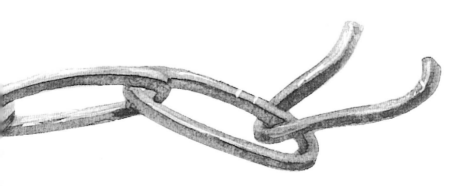

"Your husband is OK, Mrs. Folley. No problems. And I want to say hello to all of your children and tell them they should be proud of their father."

SNATCHING UP THE RING MIKE AFTER KNOCKING OUT ZORA FOLLEY, AND ADDRESSING JOELLA FOLLEY WHO SAT ANXIOUSLY AT HOME IN FRONT OF HER TV SET

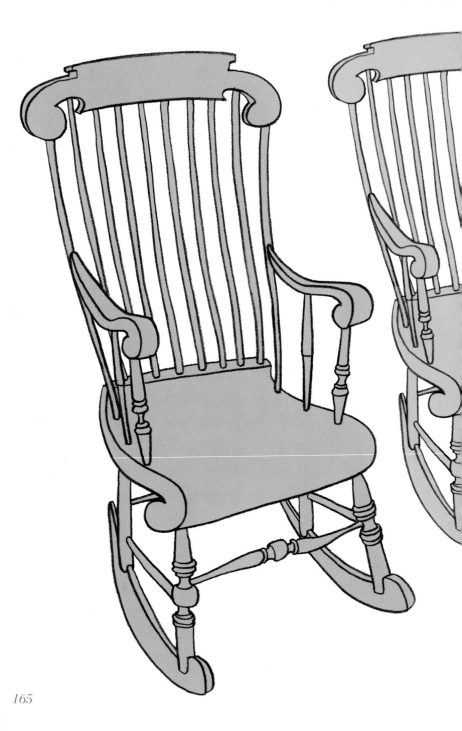

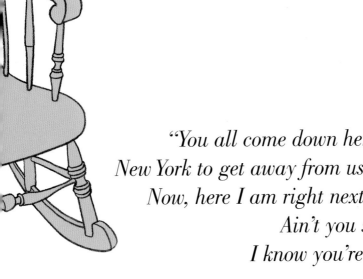

"You all come down here from New York to get away from us people. Now, here I am right next to you. Ain't you scared? I know you're scared."

ALI KIDDING AN ELDERLY JEWISH WOMAN IN MIAMI BEACH
AS THEY ROCKED IN RHYTHM IN ROCKING CHAIRS
IN FRONT OF A JEWISH COMMUNITY CENTER. (IN 1974, ALI
ARRANGED A LOAN AGAINST HIS NEXT FIGHT PURSE TO
SEND $100,000 TO PREVENT THE CLOSING OF A JEWISH SENIOR
CITIZENS' COMMUNITY CENTER IN THE BRONX WHICH
SERVED HOLOCAUST SURVIVORS.)

*"I know I got it made
while the masses of black people
are catchin' hell,
but as long as they ain't free,
I ain't free."*

"*What do I like in a woman?*
I like black girls,
and only black girls,
the darker the better.
And tall, because I'm tall,
with long shapely legs."

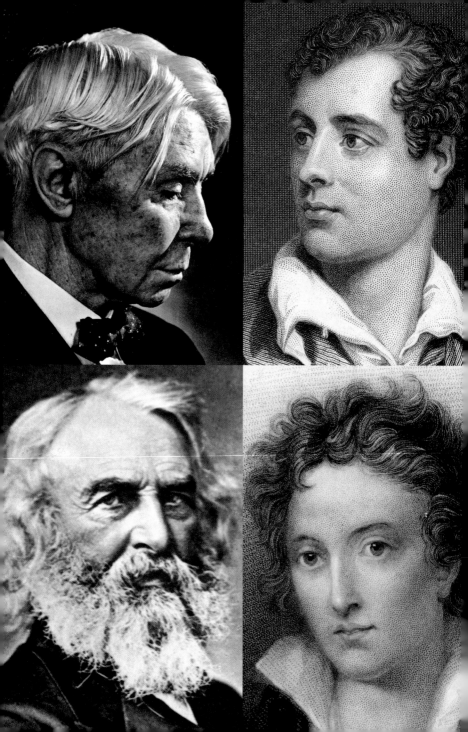

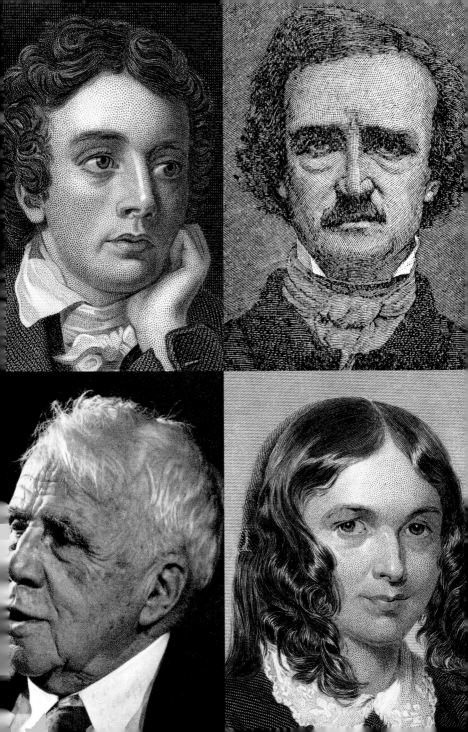

"You call my poetry horrible? I bet my poetry gets printed and quoted more than any that's been turned out by the poem writers that them critics like!"

Parks: "*Kirk Douglas in* Cast a Giant Shadow? *Paul Newman in* Harper?"

Ali: "*Naw, naw. Something rough– with ghosts. No love and sex and stuff. What's that?* Goliath and the Vampires! *That's for me, brother! Find out when it starts.*"

Parks: "*It's half over.*"
(HOPING HE WOULD BE SAVED
FROM THE VAMPIRES)

Ali: "*Come on. Let's go anyhow. The last half is always the best.*"

"Sorry, but I don't see white women."

*DROPPING A HOTEL KEY THAT
HAD BEEN SEDUCTIVELY PLACED IN HIS
HAND BY SCREEN STAR KIM NOVAK*

*"Chubby Checker
  is catching hell with
  a white woman.
  And I'm catching hell
  for NOT wanting
  a white woman."*

*"Don't ever squeeze
a fighter's hand, man.
You're doing good
just to lay your eyes on me."*

*REACTING TO AN OVERLY AGGRESSIVE
HANDSHAKE FROM A FAN*

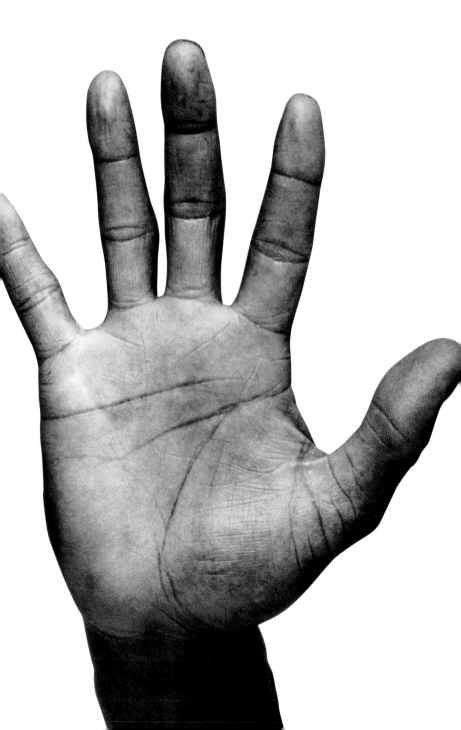

"I took care of the *Big Ugly Bear*,
Made it a habit to whop the *Rabbit*,
Punched the *Mummy* in his tummy,
And won a thrilla from the *Gorilla*.
Turned the *Washerwoman* into a girl,
And tamed the clumsy, slippery *Squirrel*.
And when I stop Shavers I'll beg his pardon,
But the place for *Acorn* to fall is the Garden.
Class dismissed."

CLAY/ALI USUALLY NICKNAMED
HIS OPPONENTS.
(FOLLOWING ARE 18 IN THE
ORDER IN WHICH
HE FOUGHT THEM.)

Archie Moore

*"The Old Man
(because he's old enough
to be my granddaddy)"*

Jean-Pierre Coopman

"The Dyin' Lion
(they call him
The Lion of Flanders, but I'm
gonna slay the Lion)"

HERAKLES SLAYING THE NEMEAN LION,
FROM A GREEK AMPHORA, 510 B.C.

Sonny Liston

*"The Big Ugly Bear
(because he's ugly
and smells like a bear)"*

Floyd Patterson

*"The Rabbit
(because a rabbit is ascared
of his own shadow)"*

George Chuvalo

"The Washerwoman
(he punches like a woman
washing clothes)"

WOMAN IRONING,
EDGAR DEGAS, 1885

Cleveland Williams

*"Krazy Kat
(they call him Big Cat,
but if he thinks he
can beat me, he's crazy)"*

Ernie Terrell

"The Octopus
(he grabs and holds
when he fights)"

Oscar Bonavena

*"The Bull
(because he looks
like a bull and his talk
is all bull)"*

Joe Frazier

"The Gorilla
(he's uglier than
King Kong)"

Jimmy Ellis

*"The Squirrel
(he can run,
but he can't hide)"*

Buster Mathis

*"The Mountain
(because he's as big
as a mountain—
and the mountain WILL come
to Muhammad!)"*

MT. FUJI,
KATSUSHIKA HOKUSAI,
1830

Jürgen Blin

"The Butcher
(he's a butcher by trade
and he cuts easy)"

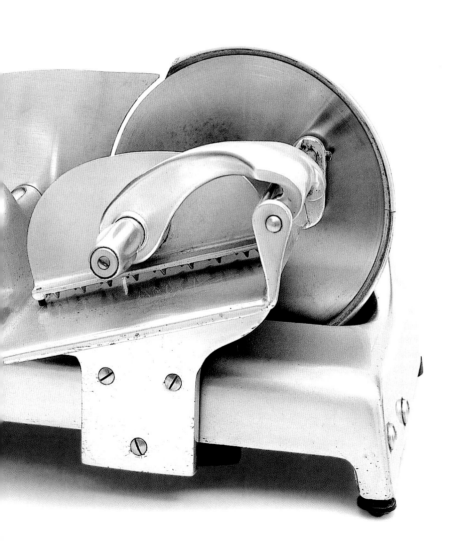

George Foreman

"The Mummy
(he IS a mummy, and
I'm going to be
the Mummy's curse)"

Chuck Wepner

*"The Bleeder
(he looks like a can of
tomato soup was
poured over his head)"*

Antonio Inoki

"The Pelican
(because he's got the biggest jaw
God ever gave a man)"

Earnie Shavers

*"The Acorn
(he's got a shaved head that
looks like an acorn)"*

Leon Spinks

"Dracula
(the man is missing
his front teeth)"

Larry Holmes

*"The Peanut
(because his head is
shaped like a peanut, and
I'm gonna shell him)"*

"I'm so fast that last night I turned the light switch off in my bedroom...

and I was
in bed before the room
was dark."

"It's been a long time
Since I put my predictions in rhythm and rhyme,
But it was Bonavena who started it all
By getting out of line.
He has asked the commission to waive
The three-knockdown rule.
He must be crazy or maybe a fool.

He couldn't have been talking
To some angel from heaven,
Now he has the nerve to predict I'll fall in eleven.
If this is his joke, it's at a bad time,
For being so rash, he'll fall in round nine.

I understand in Argentina,
The officials plainly said,
They wanted little Oscar
To shave his shaggy head.
When I start going upside his heavy mop,
Bonavena will yell, 'STOP!'"

"This is being free,
staying down to earth
and nature."

IN THE EARLY EVENING OF HIS BOUT AGAINST
OSCAR BONAVENA, ALI DESCENDED INTO THE GRIMY
SUBWAY, ARRIVED AT 34TH STREET UNDER
MADISON SQUARE GARDEN, AND HUSTLED A CROWD
OF 50 OR SO NEW YORK SUBWAY RIDERS,
CHOSEN AT RANDOM, THROUGH THE GARDEN ENTRANCE
TO SEE THE FIGHT FOR FREE.

*"He the devil.
Not enough fire in hell
for him."*

UPON HEARING OF THE DEATH OF SONNY LISTON

"At home I'm a nice guy,
   but I don't want the world to know.
   Humble people don't get very far."

"It's not bragging if you can back it up."

"Lack of faith makes people afraid
   of meeting challenges, and I believe in myself."

"Hating people because of their color is wrong
   and it doesn't matter which color
   does the hating. It's just plain wrong."

"Be loud, be pretty and keep
   their black-hatin' asses in their seats."

"You're the new man in the ghetto.
The brothers gotta be copyin' you.
Them niggers is ALL shavin' their heads."

AFTER KISSING THE BALD HEAD OF TELLY SAVALAS

TO THE GREAT NEW YORK METS PITCHER
TOM SEAVER, AN HOUR INTO DINNER
WITH SEAVER AND REPORTER DICK SCHAAP:

"Hey, you a nice fella.
Which paper you write for?"

"Jooooe Frazieeeer.
Ain't he ugly?
He's too ugly to be champion
of the world.
The Champ should be pretty,
like me."

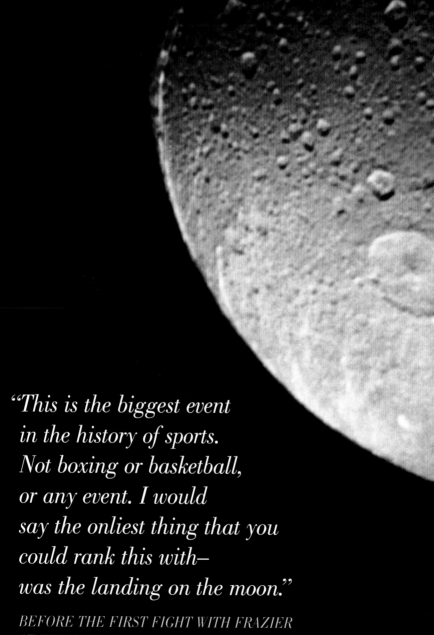

*"This is the biggest event
in the history of sports.
Not boxing or basketball,
or any event. I would
say the onliest thing that you
could rank this with—
was the landing on the moon."*

BEFORE THE FIRST FIGHT WITH FRAZIER
AT THE GARDEN

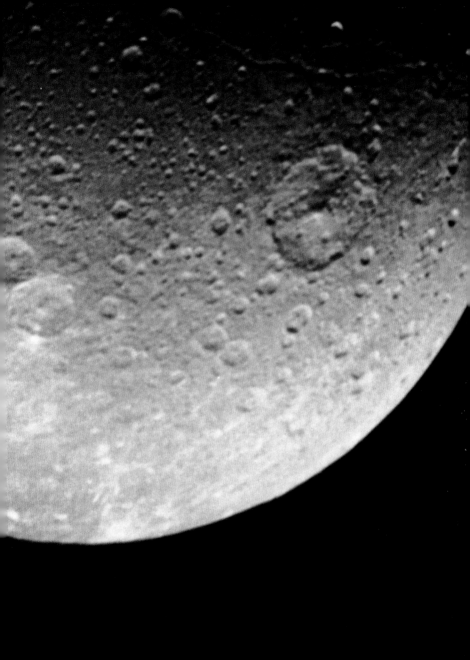

THOMAS D. RICE, A WHITE STAGE STAR IN THE MID-19TH CENTURY, PORTRAYING HIS POPULAR BLACKFACE REPRESENTATION OF "JIM CROW," A "COMIC" STEREOTYPE OF THE NEGRO IN AMERICA

*"Anybody black who thinks Frazier
can whip me is an Uncle Tom.
Everybody who's black wants me
to keep winning. I'm proving
you can be a new kind of black man."*

Ali:
"Bundini, are we going to dance?"

Drew 'Bundini' Brown:
"All night long!"

Ali:
"Yes, we're going to dance—
we're going to dance and dance!"

A PREFIGHT RITUAL
IN THE ALI DRESSING ROOM

"*I looked up, and I was on the floor.*"

ALI/FRAZIER I
ALI LOSES ON POINTS AFTER 31
CONSECUTIVE VICTORIES

"I lied."

AFTER LOSING TO FRAZIER
IN THEIR FIRST FIGHT,
ALI WAS ASKED IF HE PLANNED
TO KISS JOE'S SHOES,
SOMETHING ALI PROMISED
IN HIS PREFIGHT HYPE

*"Frazier's no real champion.
Nobody wants to talk to him. Oh, maybe
Nixon will call him if he wins.
I don't think he'll call me."*

PRESIDENT NIXON WAS OBSESSED WITH STIFLING ANTIWAR DISSENT, AND "CASSIUS CLAY" WAS "NIXON'S PET PEEVE." ACCORDING TO THE WHITE HOUSE CHIEF OF STAFF, NIXON WAS ECSTATIC AFTER ALI LOST TO FRAZIER, JUMPING UP AND DOWN CELEBRATING THE DEFEAT OF "THAT DRAFT-DODGER ASSHOLE."

*"My toughest fight
was with my first wife."*

"Ain't no reason for me

ON WHY HE HELD BACK
WHILE BEATING JIMMY ELLIS

l nobody in the ring."

"I'm gonna do to Buster...

...What the Indians did to Custer."

BEFORE FIGHTING BUSTER MATHIS

"You ain't gonna stop the fight!"

*ALI SCREAMING AT DR. FERDIE PACHECO
AFTER BEING TOLD THAT HIS JAW
HAD BEEN BROKEN BY A KEN NORTON
PUNCH IN THE FIRST ROUND*

*DREW 'BUNDINI' BROWN,
TEARS STREAMING DOWN HIS FACE
AT THE SIGHT OF THE BADLY
BROKEN JAW OF MUHAMMAD ALI,
AT THE END OF THE
DISASTROUS 12-ROUND FIGHT*

*"More people
come to see me open
a supermarket
than to see Joe Frazier
defend his
championship."*

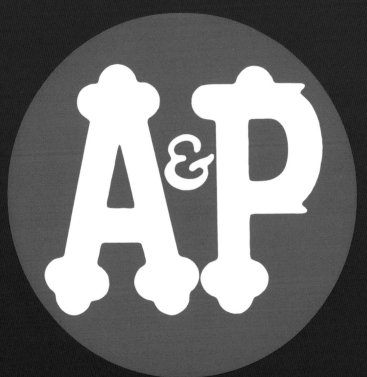

"It wouldn't smell good."

ALI EXPLAINING WHY
FRAZIER NEVER
HAD A COLOGNE NAMED
AFTER HIM

"This is dog-eat-dog, life or death."

BEFORE THE ALI/FRAZIER II FIGHT

"What you saw tonight was near to death."

AFTER A VICTORIOUS ALI AND A BEATEN FRAZIER FOUGHT FOR THEIR VERY LIVES, BOTH COMBATANTS TALKED OF THEIR NEAR-DEATH EXPERIENCE.

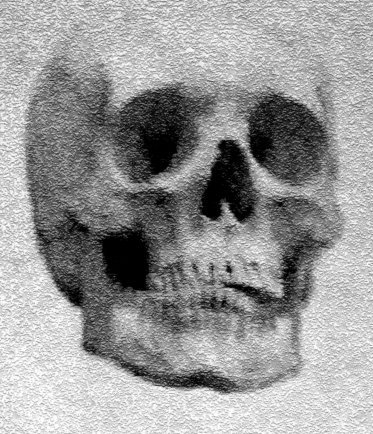

"We hit each other with shots that would take down a building."

*ALI, BARELY AUDIBLE,
THE MORNING AFTER ALI/FRAZIER II*

"Sammy Davis told me it was the most beautiful fight he had ever seen, and he only has one eye."

COMMENTING ON THE OUTCOME OF ALI/FRAZIER II

"That night, if Frazier had killed me,
I would have gotten up.
I would have become the first dead
champion in history."

REMINISCING ON WINNING BACK
HIS CHAMPIONSHIP IN
THE REMATCH WITH JOE FRAZIER

*A FABRIC-WRAPPED
BAKONGO COFFIN
(19TH CENTURY, AFRICA)*

Many people are [...]
between me and Joe [...]
It's not that, We j[...]
But we do agree [...]
that is We dedica[...]
all We can in h[...]
Rubin Hurricane[...]
Who Was unjust[...]

making this fight
izies a grudge fight.
doesn't get along.

ne thing, and
ourselves to doing

ing free

Carter, a Great Mom

imprisoned,

Muhammad Ali.

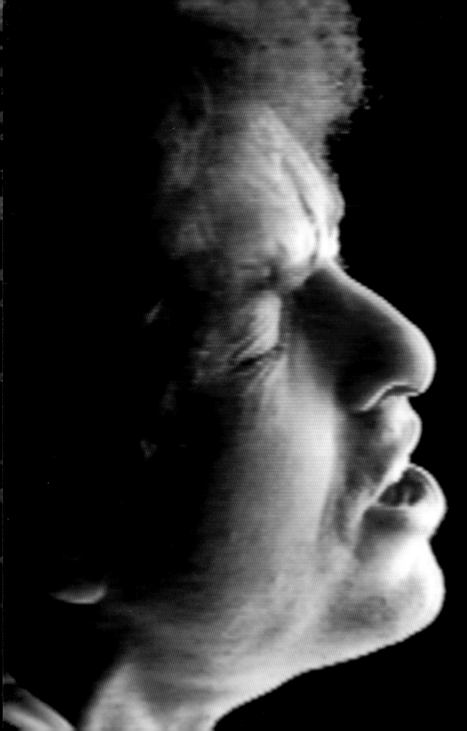

"Bob Dylan, who he?"

*ALI'S REACTION ON
BEING TOLD THAT BOB DYLAN
WAS WRITING A SONG PROTESTING
THE IMPRISONMENT OF
RUBIN 'HURRICANE' CARTER*

*"What's my greatest weakness?
    Sad stories, people with problems."*

*"The service you do for others is the rent
    you pay for your room here on Earth."*

*"He who is not courageous enough to take
    risks will accomplish nothing in life."*

**"March to prison
with me Friday."**

In the growing battle to free Hurricane Carter,
Muhammad Ali will personally lead a
People's March in Trenton, Friday, 9:30 AM!

"We march to defend the black martyr, Rubin 'Hurricane' Carter."

The only innocent Hurricane!

"**Y**ou people out there,
You all got the connection
And the complexion
To get Rubin 'Hurricane' Carter
The right protection,
Which leads to good affection."

*ALI URGING ON 20,000 SCREAMING BOB DYLAN
FANS (MOSTLY WHITE) AT
A MADISON SQUARE GARDEN
BENEFIT CONCERT*

*UPON MEETING
FELLOW ACTIVIST
BOB DYLAN FOR
THE FIRST TIME
THAT NIGHT,
ALI SAID TO THE
AUDIENCE:*

Night of the
Hurricane!

"*Dylan ain't as
purty as me,
you'll have to admit.*"

*"There's the doorbell.
Must be some kids—
wanna see some magic tricks again."*

ALI PERFORMED SLEIGHT-OF-HAND
MAGIC TRICKS FOR ANY AND ALL TO SEE,
EVEN PUTTING ON A SHOW IN THE
LOBBY OF HIS HOTEL ON THE MORNING
OF A BIG FIGHT.

HIPPODROME THEATRE BALTIMORE

WEEK STARTS FRI. NOV. 13

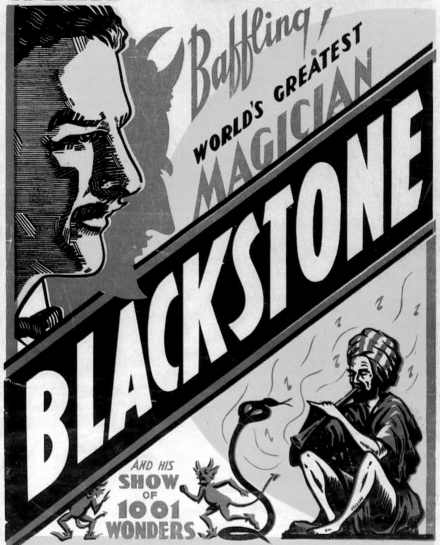

Baffling!

WORLD'S GREATEST MAGICIAN

BLACKSTONE

AND HIS SHOW OF 1001 WONDERS

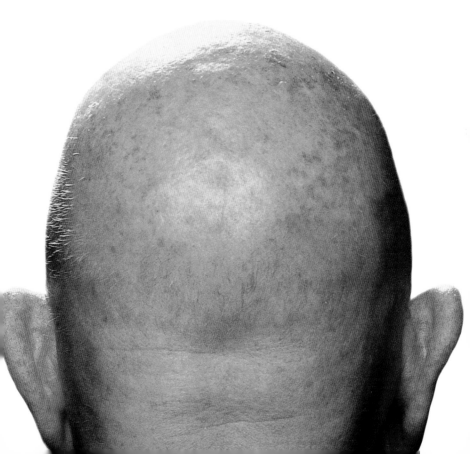

"*I'll give
a thousand dollars to anyone
who brings me
Howard Cosell's toupee.*"

ALI TO AN AUDIENCE OF COLLEGE STUDENTS

"**I**'m gonna let everybody know
That thing you got on your head is a phony,
And it comes from the tail of a pony!"

MUHAMMAD ALI
TO HOWARD COSELL

*"Howard Cosell was gonna
be a boxer when he was a kid–
only they couldn't find
a mouthpiece big enough."*

*"Sometimes Howard makes me wish
I was a dog
and he was a fireplug."*

PERSEUS WITH THE HEAD OF MEDUSA,
ANTONIO CANOVA, 1805

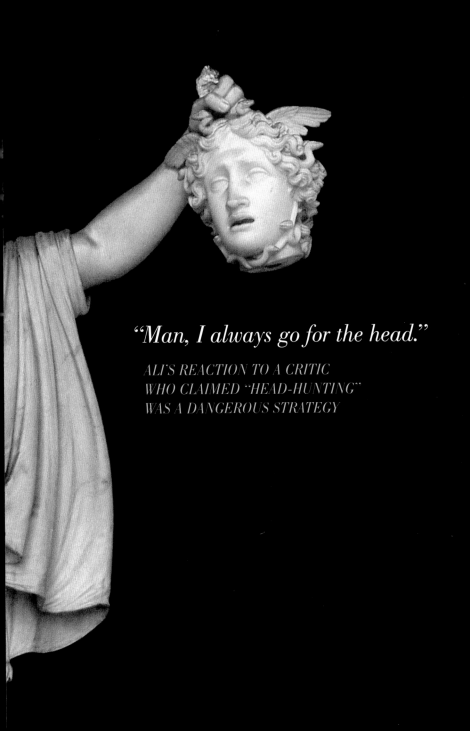

"Man, I always go for the head."

ALI'S REACTION TO A CRITIC
WHO CLAIMED "HEAD-HUNTING"
WAS A DANGEROUS STRATEGY

*"It's you! It's you!
I knew you would be here.
My mom said no, but it's you!"*

Ali: "Well, who am I?"

Boy: "You're Muhammad Ali.
Champion of the World. The greatest ever."

Ali: "Does your mom feel that way too?"

Boy: "Naw, she says you're just another nigger."

(AFTER A DEAFENING PAUSE)

Ali: "I never heard that word before.
What's it mean?"

Boy: "It's short for Negro."

(ALI'S LAUGHTER LIT UP THE DINING ROOM!)

Jack Johnson
Jack Dempsey
Joe Louis

TO LARRY KING OF CNN,
WHO ASKED ALI IF HE REALLY THOUGHT
HE WAS THE GREATEST EVER:

"Of course not.
How would I know who the
greatest fighter was.
How can you compare fighters
from different eras?
I was probably the best of my time but
how do I know what would
have happened if I fought Louis,
Dempsey or Jack Johnson.
Who knows?"

"*You know what
Abraham Lincoln said
after he came off
a two-day drunk?
'I freed the whoooo?!'*"

WHAT ARE YOUR FAVORITE OBJECTS?

"Automobiles and mirrors."

232

GOAT, *AN ACRONYM*
FOR GREATEST OF ALL TIME,
IS USED BY ALI IN
HIS BUSINESS AFFAIRS.

"WOW.
I can't believe it's
really John Travolta
coming into
MY house to see ME!"

Howard Cosell:

"You seem awfully truculent today, Champ."

tru·cu·lent \-lənt\ *adj* [L *trucule*
to MIr *trú* doomed person] (ca.
ity : CRUEL, SAVAGE **2** : DEADL
: VITRIOLIC **4** : aggressively sel
lent·ly *adv*

Muhammad Ali:
"I don't know what truculent means,
but if it's good, it's me."

, fr. *truc-*, *trux* savage; perh. akin
) **1** : feeling or displaying feroc-
ESTRUCTIVE **3** : scathingly harsh
ertive : BELLIGERENT — **tru·cu-**

Ali Bo

maye!

(Ali Kill Him!)

ALI LEADING THOUSANDS OF
CHANTING FANS IN ZAIRE
BEFORE THE RUMBLE IN THE JUNGLE

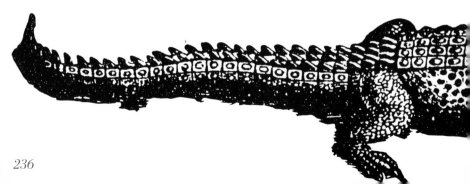

"You think the world was shocked
When Nixon resigned?
Wait till I whup
George Foreman's behind.
I done something new for this fight,
I done rassled with an alligator!
That's right,
I have rassled with an alligator!
I done tussled with a whale!
I done handcuffed lightning,
Throwed thunder in jail!
Only last week I murdered a rock,
Injured a stone,
Hospitalized a brick,
I'm so mean I make medicine sick."

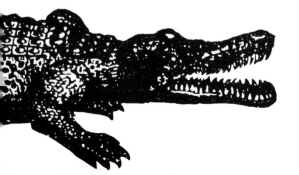

"*I've seen
George Foreman
shadowboxing...
and the shadow won.*"

"**D**on King's body
did four years in prison,
But his hair
Got the chair."

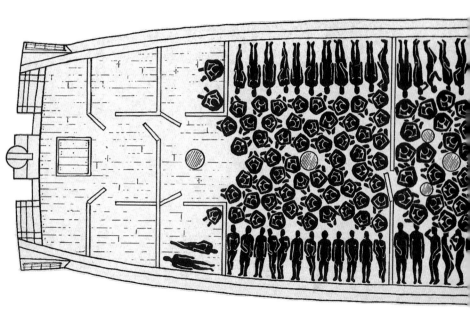

12 MILLION AFRICANS WERE KIDNAPPED AND MADE SLAVES IN AMERICA.

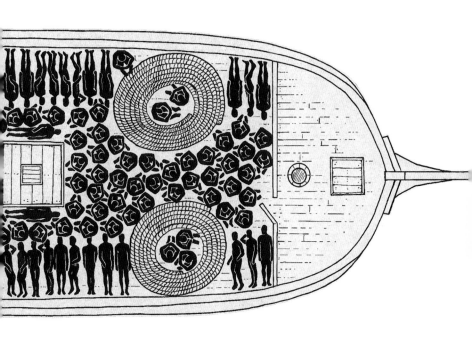

"From the slave ship To the championship."

THIS CONTROVERSIAL SLOGAN FROM DON KING
PROMOTED THE CHAMPIONSHIP BOUT BETWEEN
TWO AFRICAN-AMERICAN CHAMPIONS.
WHEN PRESIDENT MOBUTU OF ZAIRE SAW POSTERS
WITH THE SLOGAN, HE ORDERED THEM BURNED.

"War...War...War."

ALI POUNDING ON DRUMS IN KINSHASA, ZAIRE,
SHOUTING WITH EACH BEAT,
BEFORE WINNING BACK HIS CHAMPIONSHIP
FROM GEORGE FOREMAN

*"If I win,
I'm going to be the
black Kissinger.
I'm not just a fighter,
I'm a world figure."*

FEATS
OF
CLAY

Dundee: "Don Waldheim."

Ali: "A nobody."

Dundee: "Fred Askew."

Ali: "A nobody."

Dundee: "Sylvester Dullaire."

Ali: "A nobody."

Dundee: "Chuck Wepner."

Ali: "Nobody."

Dundee: "John Carroll."

Ali: "Nobody."

Dundee: "Cookie Wallace."

Ali: "Nobody."

Dundee: "Gary 'Hobo' Wiler."

Ali: "A tramp."

Dundee: "Vernon Clay."

Ali (hesitating): "Vernon Clay?!
He might be good."

*"All you boys who think
George Foreman is gonna whup me...
when you get to Africa,
Mobutu's people are gonna put you in a pot,
cook you and eat you."*

*ALI SPOOFING THE RACIST CONCEPT OF AFRICAN TRIBALISM
(MOBUTU SESE SEKO WAS THE DICTATOR OF ZAIRE)*

*"A man should never,
ever, eat poke.
I can't let Foreman win.
He eats pork chops."*

"You have heard of me since you were young. You have been following me since you were a little boy. Now, you must meet me, your master."

ALI IN THE CENTER OF THE RING DURING PREFIGHT INSTRUCTIONS, HYPNOTICALLY WHISPERING TO GEORGE FOREMAN

"Shut up, I know I'm doing."

ALI'S RESPONSE
TO HIS CORNERMEN,
WHO WERE SCREAMING
"ARE YOU CRAZY!"
D "STAY THE FUCK AWAY
FROM THE ROPES,"
URING HIS ROPE-A-DOPE

ON THE ROPES FOR ALMOST EIGHT FULL ROUNDS,
FEIGNING HELPLESSNESS, ALI SUDDENLY TURNED
PUNCHED-OUT GEORGE FOREMAN AND KO'D HIM.
CALLY DUBBED HIS STRATEGY "THE ROPE-A-DOPE."

up, what doing!"

"When I beat Sonny Liston,
  I shocked the world.
  When I joined the Muslims,
  I shocked the world.
  When I beat George Foreman,
  I shocked the world.
  I am from the House of Shock!"

"The bull is stronger...

...but the matador is smarter."

TALKING ABOUT THE
ROPE-A-DOPE

"I watched a horror movie, The Blood Baron, which really scared me. Compared to that, beating George Foreman was just another day in the gym."

A 12ᵀᴴ–15ᵀᴴ CENTURY IFÈ BRONZE MASTERPIECE FROM THE YÒRUBÁ PEOPLE OF NIGERIA

"Africa is the home of the Original Man, the black man, and that Africa, where the slaves were stolen from, has all kinds of rich history."

"So what if I am the first
black athlete to stand up and
say what I feel!
Hate! Hate! Hate!
Who's got time to go around
hatin' whites all day?
I don't hate tigers either—
but I know they'll bite!"

"Who was lynched?
Were we the ones to burn crosses,
did we tar and feather,
rape, hang, beat up with sticks,
did we enslave a people?
Who were slaves for 400 years?
What did we ever do to
America's white people that they
now claim we hate them?"

Ali: "I told you I was gonna whup
George Foreman.
Well, I'm back from Zaire and
I did whup George Foreman,
and now you're gonna whup cancer!"

Boy: "No, Muhammad.
I'm going to meet God.
And I'm going to tell Him I know you."

WHEN MUHAMMAD ALI AND JOE BUGNER
SELECTED THE BOXING GLOVES THEY
WOULD WEAR IN THEIR TITLE BOUT, THE
MALAYSIAN BOXING COMMISSION
PLACED THE GLOVES IN SEPARATE BOXES
AND SEALED THEM WITH MELTED WAX

Ali: "*Where they gonna
put the gloves?*"

Commissioner: "*We will put them in prison—
for security.*"

Ali: "*They didn't kill nobody—yet.
They might have to go
to jail after. I been boxing
20 years and I ain't
never seen gloves in a jail.
The poor gloves.
The gloves need a lawyer.*"

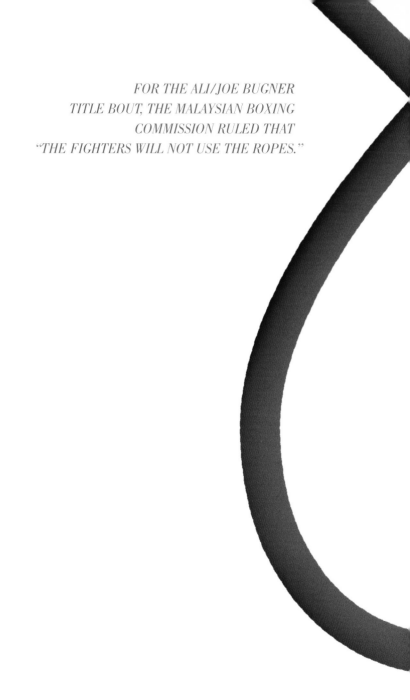

*FOR THE ALI/JOE BUGNER
TITLE BOUT, THE MALAYSIAN BOXING
COMMISSION RULED THAT
"THE FIGHTERS WILL NOT USE THE ROPES."*

"I can't use the ropes?
I can't use the Rope-a-Dope?
I won't HANG him!"

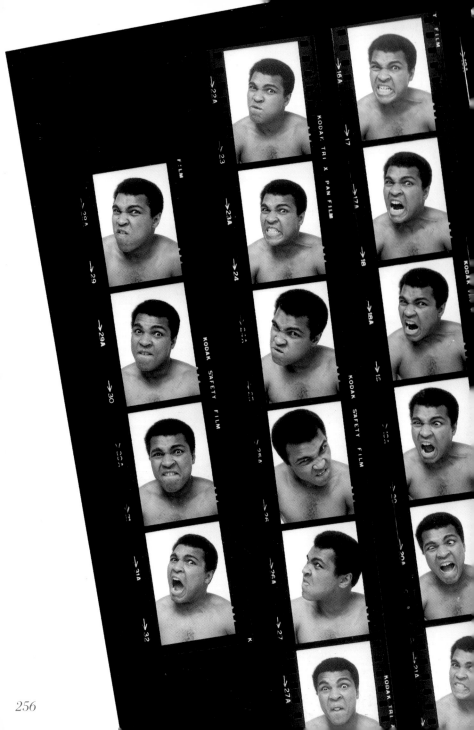

256

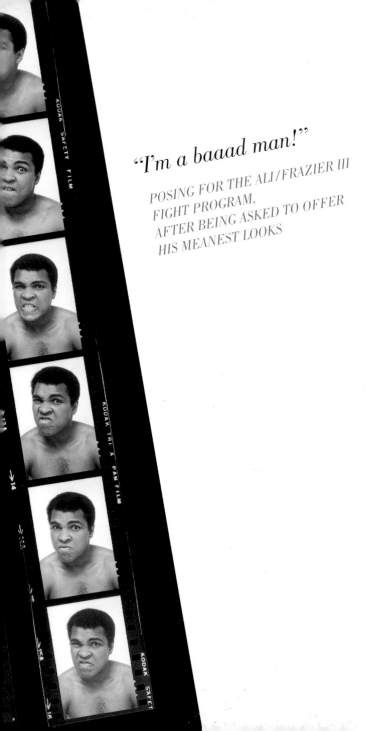

"*I'm a baaad man!*"

POSING FOR THE ALI/FRAZIER III
FIGHT PROGRAM,
AFTER BEING ASKED TO OFFER
HIS MEANEST LOOKS

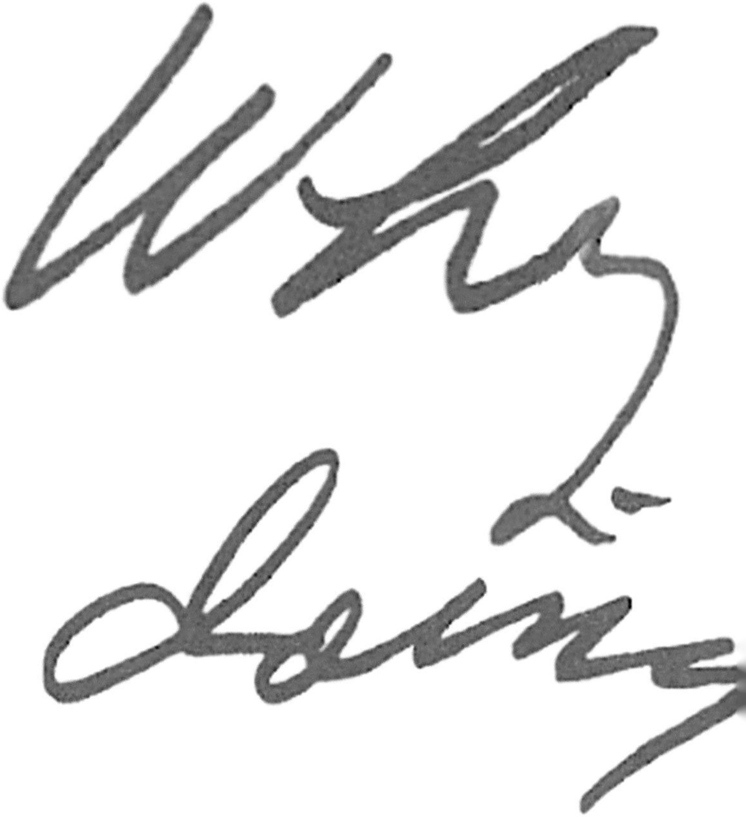

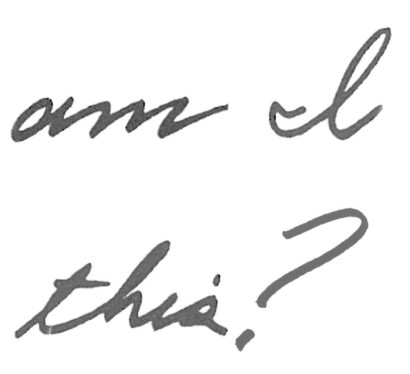

*"What am I doin' here against
this beast of a man?
It's so painful. I must be crazy.
I always bring out the best in the men I fight,
but Joe Frazier, I'll tell the world right now,
brings out the best in me.
I'm gonna tell ya, that's one helluva man,
and God bless him."*

"I didn't know who Bob Dylan was. But he came out of nowhere to give a protest concert for Rubin 'Hurricane' Carter. The words to his songs are poetry—like a prophet from the Bible."

"Fidel Castro is a man with his own beliefs, a man you've got to admire for taking a stand like he did for what he believed."

"Malcolm X said courageous things,
wasn't afraid of nothing.
    He wasn't just a great black man.
    He was a great man."

"President Kennedy was
an inspiration,
not just to the young
people of America,
but the whole world.
His assassination changed history."

IT WILL BE A
AND A
AND A
WHEN I GET THE
IN

KILLER
CHILLER
THRILLA
GORILLA
MANILA

THE THRILLA IN MANILA, 1975

Ali comes out to meet Frazier,
But Frazier starts to retreat,
If Frazier goes back an inch further,
He'll wind up in a ringside seat,
Ali swings with a left, Ali swings with a right,
Look at the kid carry the fight.

Frazier keeps duckin'
But there's not enough room,
It's a matter of time
Before Ali lowers the boom.
Now Ali lands with a right,
What a beautiful swing,
But the punch lifts Frazier
Clean out of the ring.
Frazier's still risin'
But the referee wears a frown,
'Cause he can't start countin'
'Til Frazier comes down.

Now Frazier disappears from view,
The crowd is getting frantic,
Our radar stations have picked him up,
He's somewhere over the Atlantic.
Who would have thought
When they came to the fight,
That they would witness
The launching of a black satellite?

Yes, the crowd did not dream
When they laid down their money,
That Ali would retire
Frazier and Sonny.
Frazier came out smoking,
And Ali wasn't joking.
He was peckin' and a pokin',
Pourin' water on his smokin'.
This might shock and amaze ya,
I'm gonna destroy Joe Frazier."

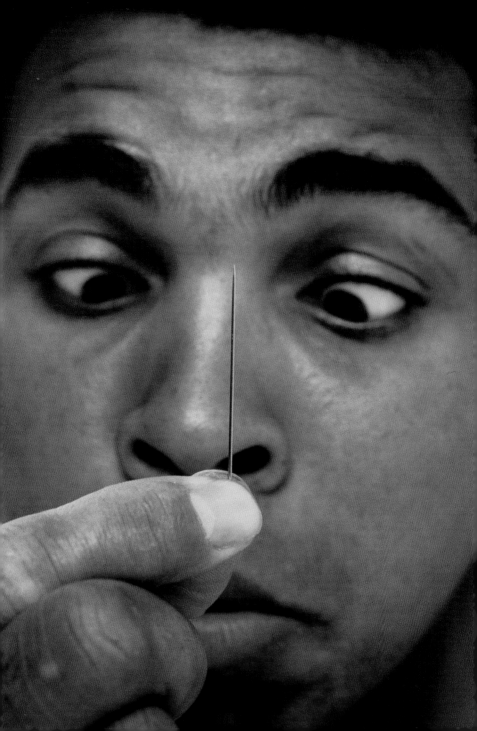

"I got some last words for Joe Frazier.
I got a balloon punch and a needle punch.
The balloon punch is a left jab which
swells him up, blows him up, puffs him up.
And the needle gonna bust him.
That's the right hand. Whop!"

BEFORE ALI/FRAZIER III

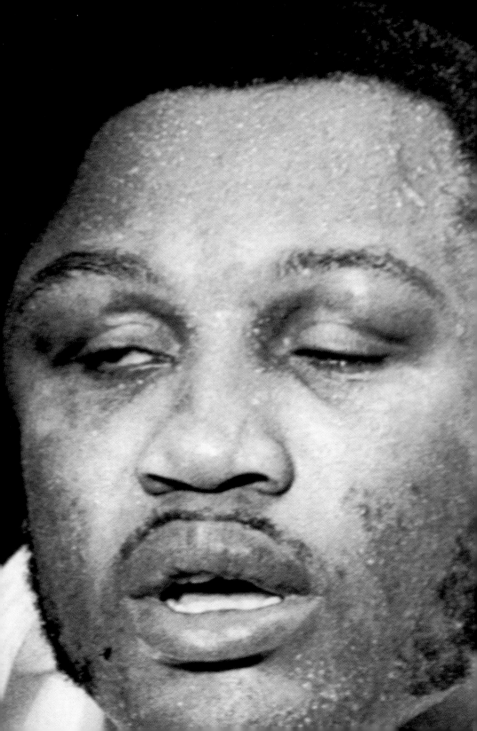

"Got nothin' against Frazier personally,
I'm just earnin' a livin.'
After that, he can go back to his
diamond rings and his Cadillacs.
But I called him ignorant 14 times.
He made an ignorant statement.
He said he beat me so bad
the first fight I had to go to the hospital.
I went to check my jaw to see if it was broke.
It was swollen, but it was OK.
Ain't that ignorant?
Why did he make that statement?
But HE stayed in the hospital 30 days
in intensive care.
He took a hell of a head whuppin.'
So he's gonna fall.
This will be a knockout for sure."

> *"What you got in that niggah head? Fuckin' rock?!"*
>
> *ALI SHOUTING TO FRAZIER DURING THE THRILLA IN MANILA*

*"What's holding
this mothafuckin' fool up?!"*

FRAZIER TO HIS
CORNER AFTER ROUND 10

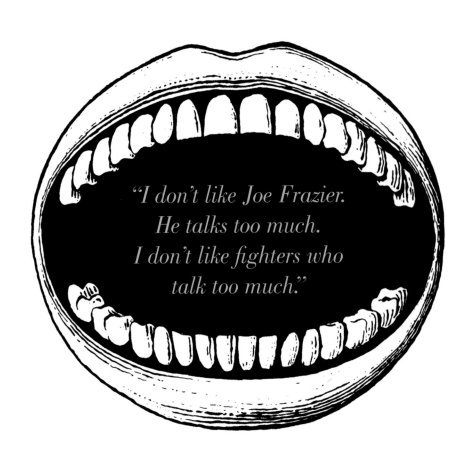

"I don't like Joe Frazier.
He talks too much.
I don't like fighters who
talk too much."

*"I said a lot of things
in the heat of the moment that
I shouldn't have said.
Called him names I shouldn't
have called him.
I apologize for that. I'm sorry.
It was all meant to promote the fight."*

APOLOGIZING TO JOE FRAZIER IN 2001

"Take my advice.
Get a gun."

*TO MIDDLEWEIGHT
ROY JONES JR.,
AFTER A MOCK
SPARRING SESSION
WITH ALI*

Howard Cosell:
"Muhammad, you clearly aren't
the same fighter you were ten years ago."

Muhammad Ali:
"Well, Howard, I just talked to your wife
and she says you're not the
same man you were TWO years ago."

"Don't want people who don't like me treadin' on my name."

MUHAMMAD ALI WAS AWARDED A STAR ON HOLLYWOOD'S WALK OF FAME; BUT, UNLIKE OTHERS SET INTO THE HOLLYWOOD BOULEVARD PAVEMENT, ALI'S STAR WAS MOUNTED—AT HIS REQUEST—INTO THE WALL OF THE NEARBY KODAK THEATRE.

*"I've seen the whole world.
I learned somethin' from people everywhere.
There's truth in Hinduism, Christianity,
Islam, all religions.
And in just plain talkin.'
The only religion that matters,
is the real religion–love."*

"I wish people would love everybody else the way they love me. It would be a better world."

ASKED IF HE'D EVER BEEN IN LOVE:

"Not with anybody else."

FREEDOM

ROAD

THE WAR WAS DONE—THE LONG AND BLOODY STRUGGLE THAT was, at the time, the greatest people's war the world had ever known—and the men in blue marched home. The men in gray, stunned and hurt, looked about at their land, and saw what war does.

At Appomattox Court House, General Lee laid down his arms, and then it was all finished. And in the warm southland, there were four million black men who were free. A hard-won freedom, a precious thing. A free man counts tomorrow and yesterday, and both of them are his; hunger and there's no master to feed you, but walk with long steps and no master says go slowly. Two hundred thousand of these black men were soldiers of the republic when the struggle finished, and many of them went home with guns in their hands.

Gideon Jackson was one of them. Tall and strong and tired, a gun in his hand and a faded blue uniform on his back, he came home to the Carolina soil and the Carwell Plantation. The big white house stood much as he remembered it, not damaged by the war, but the gardens and fields were weeds and jungle, and the Carwells had gone away— none knew where. The freedmen, as they returned, took up their lives in the old slave quarters, together with those who had never gone away. And as the months passed, more and more of the freedmen returned to the Carwell Plantation, from the cold northland where they had gone to find freedom, from the ranks of the Union Army, and from their hiding places in the piney woods and the lonesome swamps. They took up their lives with the deep wonder that they were free.

"*I don't have time to read a book–
it takes too long.*"

ON THE SET OF FREEDOM ROAD,
*STARRING MUHAMMAD ALI AS GIDEON JACKSON
(AN ESCAPED SLAVE AND RETURNING
UNION ARMY SOLDIER), WHEN ASKED IF HE
HAD READ THE BOOK BY HOWARD FAST*

*"I was the onliest boxer in history
people asked questions like a senator."*

MOSES, BY REMBRANDT

"I'm the most recognized and loved man that ever lived 'cause there weren't no satellites when Moses and Jesus were around, so people far away in the villages didn't know about them."

JESUS. BY REMBRANDT

*"I am the astronaut of boxing.
Joe Louis and Jack Dempsey were
just jet pilots.
I'm in a world of my own."*

"I'm happy because I'm free.
I've made the stand all black people
are gonna have to make
sooner or later, whether or not
they can stand up to the master."

186,000 AFRICAN-AMERICANS
JOINED THE UNION ARMY;
38,000 WERE KILLED DURING THE WAR
AGAINST THE CONFEDERACY.

TO PRESIDENT GERALD FORD IN THE OVAL OFFICE,
WHEN ALI WAS INVITED TO THE WHITE HOUSE
FOR THE FIRST TIME:

"You made a big mistake letting me come,
because now I'm going after your job."

PRESIDENT FORD ATE (JIM) CROW
FOR THE U.S. GOVERNMENT'S PAST ACTIONS
AGAINST MUHAMMAD ALI BY SAYING,
"I NEVER JOINED THE CRITICS WHO COMPLAINED ABOUT
WHAT ALI DID AND DIDN'T DO DURING
THE VIETNAM WAR. I ACCEPTED HIS DECISION...
HE WAS A MAN OF PRINCIPLE."

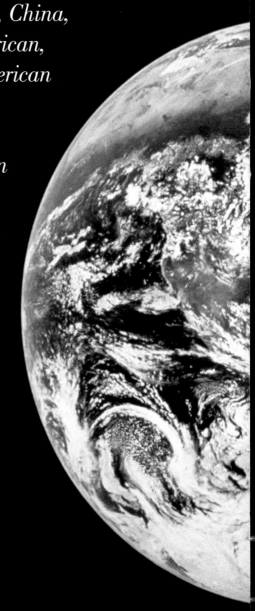

*"You can go to Japan, China,
all the European, African,
Arab, and South American
countries, and man,
they know me.
I can't name a nation
where they don't
know me."*

ALI TO A CAUCASIAN FRIEND:

"*You get in back; I'll drive.
It'll be like* Driving Miss Daisy.*"*

*"I'm the first world champion
that ever toured the world
he was champion of."*

"I was the Elvis of boxing."

"Listen, Bro, who do you think you are?
If you can't find time to sign
your name for the little guys, you don't
deserve to be called 'great'!
He and thousands of others like him have
made you what you are today.
If it hadn't been for him and those other
thousands you probably couldn't
even afford to pick up the check
for this dinner."

CHASTISING BASEBALL GREAT REGGIE JACKSON,
WHO HAD RUDELY WAVED OFF A WAITER
SEEKING AN AUTOGRAPH AT A DINNER JACKSON
WAS HOSTING

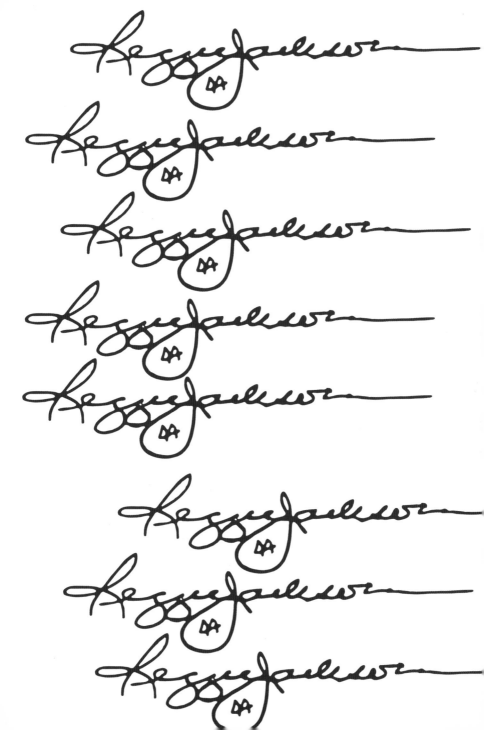

"People have died by the thousands since my case. Good people. There's so much dying that's been bigger than mine. Martin Luther King. The Kennedys. Poverty, disasters, murders, wars. Why should I matter so much? It's because of what I stand for."

ESQUIRE *COVER, OCTOBER 1968,* CREATED BY GEORGE LOIS

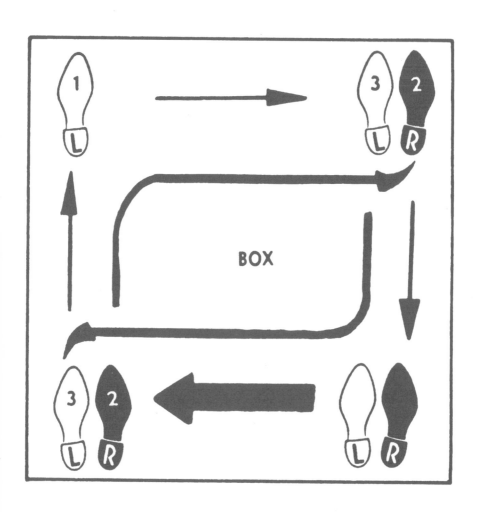

BOX

"*In the ring I can stay*
Until I'm old and gray
Because I know how to hit
And dance away."

"I'm not what I used to be."

IN DETERIORATING HEALTH,
AFTER NARROWLY DEFEATING
EARNIE SHAVERS

"I won the title, became champion.
Powerful and strong.
And then God tries you, takes my health.
Fixes it so it's hard to talk.
Hard to walk.
I'm blessed and thankful to God that
I understand he's trying me.
This is a trial from God.
He gave me this illness to remind me
that I'm not number one; He is."

ALI REFLECTING ON BEING AFFLICTED
BY PARKINSON'S DISEASE

*"Horses get old,
cars get old,
the pyramids of Egypt
are crumbling."*

ON RETIRING

"Foreman was a sore loser at the time, blaming my win on everything he could think of. But I like George today— I even use his grill."

LLINGER

*"Lonnie and I named our son
Asaad Amin Ali.
It means
'Son of the Lion.'"*

*"My left hand was shaking
because of Parkinson's,
my right hand was shaking
from fear.
Somehow, between the two of them,
I got the thing lit."*

ALI REFLECTING ON HIS TRIUMPHANT
LIGHTING OF THE OLYMPIC TORCH AT THE
1996 GAMES IN ATLANTA

Muhammad Ali.

1975

Muhammad Ali

1996

"*Killing like that can never be justified.
It's unbelievable. I could never support
hurting innocent men, women and children.
Islam is a religion of peace.*

WALL OF PRAYERS

*It does not support terrorism or killing people.
They are racist fanatics who
call themselves Muslims, permitting this
murder of thousands.''*

A FEW HOURS AFTER THE 9/11 TERRORIST ATTACKS

"Some people who call themselves Muslims do bad crazy things. But some people who call themselves Christians joined the Ku Klux Klan, lynched black people, and burned crosses on lawns. True Christianity teaches brotherhood and love, and true Islam teaches those things too. God created all people, no matter what their religion."

ON THE MORNING OF SEPTEMBER 11, 2001

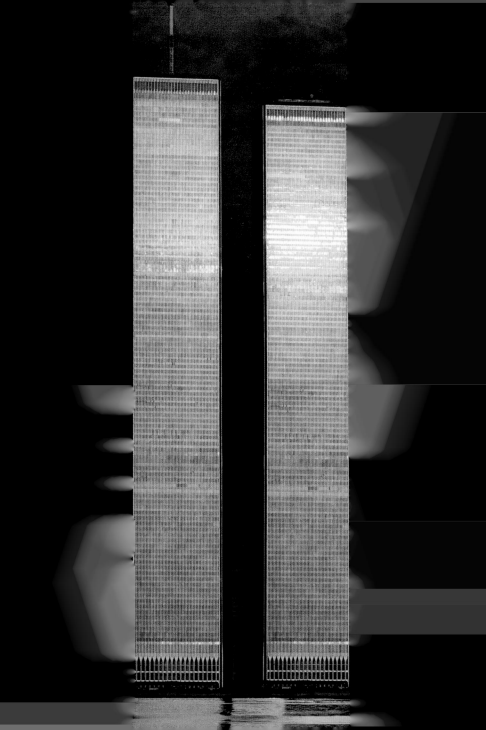

"I'm a Muslim.
I have been a Muslim for 20 years.
You know me. I'm a boxer.
I've been called the greatest.
People recognize me for being a boxer
and a man of truth.
I think all people should know the truth,
come to recognize the truth.
Islam is peace."

TEN DAYS AFTER 9/11,
AT A BROADCAST TELETHON
FOR VICTIMS OF THE
WORLD TRADE CENTER ATTACKS

*"I'm not that pretty anymore.
Now I'm just a Black Clark Gable."*

MUHAMMAD ALI, 2003

"FROM NOW ON…

*AFTER LONNIE MADE A LOVELY ACCEPTANCE SPEECH
WHEN HER HUSBAND RECEIVED AN HONORARY
DOCTORATE FROM COLUMBIA UNIVERSITY IN 1999,
A DEBILITATED MUHAMMAD ALI STOOD UP,
AND IN THE STRONGEST VOICE HE COULD MUSTER,
GAVE A SIX-WORD SPEECH TO THE ENTHRALLED
STUDENT BODY:*

CALL ME DOCTOR."

WHEN ASKED HOW HE FELT
WHEN HE WATCHED HIS DAUGHTER, LAILA ALI,
FIGHT IN THE BOXING RING:

"It's hard to watch. She's good, alright.
But a woman wasn't made
to be punched like that, especially
in the chest. I just can't watch."

WHEN ASKED IN 2003
WHAT THE BIGGEST THRILL
OF HIS CAREER WAS:

"Zaire.
Foreman.
Got my title back.
In Africa."

A 19TH CENTURY BAKONGO FETISH (NKISI)
FROM ZAIRE: A MAGICAL ANCESTOR
OBJECT OF SUPERNATURAL POWER, USED DURING
THERAPEUTIC CEREMONIES AND
FOR INVOKING DIVINE PROTECTION

"Maybe there will come a day when instead of saying 'God Bless America' everyone everywhere will say 'God Bless the World.'"

WITHALIGHTFROMABOV

STOTHEPRAIRIESTOTHE

AMGODBLESSAMERICA

CREDITS

Any omissions for copyright or credit are unintentional and appropriate credit will be given in future editions if such copyright holders contact the publisher.

Spine/Title page © 2005 Howard L. Bingham. All rights reserved. **Preface** Photograph © Carl Fischer **Introduction** Photograph © David Turnley **2** © Gloria-Leigh Logan/www.acclaimimages.com **5** Art by Luke Lois **6** © Christie's Images Ltd. 1997 **9** © Flip Schulke **10** Photograph by Luke Lois **12** Art by George Lois **14** Marvin Newman/SPORTS ILLUSTRATED **17** Theo Ehret **18** Art by Luke Lois **20** Thomas Hoepker/Magnum Photos **22** Thomas Hoepker/Magnum Photos **24** Art by Luke Lois **27** © Flip Schulke **31** © Christie's Images Ltd. 1997 **35** Art by George Lois **36** Photo by Bob Gomel/Time & Life Pictures/Getty Images **38** Art by Luke Lois **40** © Bettmann/CORBIS **42** Photograph by Luke Lois **43 left** Art by Luke Lois **45** Photographer Timothy Galfas **47** © 2005 Howard L. Bingham. All rights reserved. **50** © Hank Kaplan Boxing Archives **54** Photograph by David King, London **55** Art by Luke Lois **56** Photograph © Carl Fischer **57** Photograph by Luke Lois **58** © Steve Schapiro courtesy of Fahey/Klein Gallery **65** Photograph by Luke Lois **67** Conceived by George Lois, Photograph © Carl Fischer **70** Photograph © Carl Fischer **75** Photograph by Luke Lois **76** Thomas Hoepker/Magnum Photos **79** Photograph by Neil Leifer **80** Photo by Herb Scharfman/Time & Life Pictures/Getty Images **85** Art by Luke Lois **88** Art by Luke Lois **90** © Bettmann/CORBIS **92** Art by James Montgomery Flagg, Photo by Carl Fischer, Composition by Luke Lois **93** Thomas Hoepker/Magnum Photos **95** Photograph by Luke Lois **96** Photograph by Luke Lois **98** Photograph by Prof. Andrew Davidhazy (RIT) **99** Photograph by Neil Leifer **102** Thomas Hoepker/Magnum Photos **103** Photograph © Carl Fischer **104** Art by Luke Lois **105** © 2005 Andy Warhol Foundation for the Visual Arts/ARS, New York **106 left** Photo by Paul Schutzer/Time & Life Pictures/Getty Images **107** Art by George Lois **109** © 1980 GUNTHER/MPTV.NET **110** Photograph © Carl Fischer **113 left** Photograph © Carl Fischer **118** Photograph by Neil Leifer **119** Thomas Hoepker/Magnum Photos **123 left** Photograph by Neil Leifer **125** Photograph by Luke Lois **126** Thomas Hoepker/Magnum Photos **128** From *The Devil in Design: The Krampus Postcards* © 2004 **129** Director & Cinematographer: Timothy Galfas **132 left** © Allan Tannenbaum **133** Thomas Hoepker/Magnum Photos **134** Art by Luke Lois **136** Photograph © Carl Fischer **138** Art by Luke Lois